# GERMAN FAIRY TALES

Most people's knowledge of German fairy tales is confined to the stories written down by the brothers Grimm, of which there are many selections available. For this book, however, Maurice and Pamela Michael have carefully sifted through the enormous heritage of traditional German stories for children, and have gathered a varied and charming collection of little-known folk-tales which have been handed down among the country people of Germany for generations. They have avoided the Grimm stories because they are so well known; and if one or two of the tales in this book have a look of Grimm about them, it is because they are descended from the same source as that from which the Grimm brothers drew.

Old tales improve in the re-telling, and these lively, eventful stories are ideal for reading aloud and will delight audiences of all ages.

*Also in this series:*

BURMESE AND THAI FAIRY TALES
*by Eleanor Brockett*
CELTIC FAIRY TALES
*by Joseph Jacobs, ed. by Lucia Turnbull*
CHINESE FAIRY TALES
*by Leslie Bonnett*
DANISH FAIRY TALES
*by Inge Hack*
ENGLISH FAIRY TALES
*by Joseph Jacobs*
FAIRY TALES FROM BOHEMIA
*by Maurice and Pamela Michael*
FAIRY TALES FROM SWITZERLAND
*by Roger Duvoisin*
FAMOUS FAIRY TALES OF THE WORLD
*A selection from the series by Juliet Piggott*
FRENCH FAIRY TALES
*by Roland Gant*
GREEK FAIRY TALES
*by Barbara Ker Wilson*
INDIAN FAIRY TALES
*by Lucia Turnbull*
ITALIAN FAIRY TALES
*by Peter Lum*
JAPANESE FAIRY TALES
*by Juliet Piggott*
NORWEGIAN FAIRY TALES
*by Gert Strindberg*
PERSIAN FAIRY TALES
*by Eleanor Brockett*
POLISH FAIRY TALES
*by Zoë Zajdler*
PORTUGUESE FAIRY TALES
*by Pamela and Maurice Michael*
RUSSIAN FAIRY TALES
*by E. M. Almedingen*
SPANISH FAIRY TALES
*by John Marks*
SWEDISH FAIRY TALES
*by Irma Kaplan*
TURKISH FAIRY TALES
*by Eleanor Brockett*

# German Fairy Tales

SELECTED FROM STORIES OTHER
THAN THOSE BY THE BROTHERS GRIMM

*Translated and retold by*
MAURICE AND PAMELA MICHAEL

*Illustrated by*
HAZEL COOK

FREDERICK MULLER

*First published in Great Britain 1958
by Frederick Muller Ltd., Fleet Street, London, E.C.4.*

*Copyright © Frederick Muller, 1958*

*Reprinted 1959, 1960, 1963, 1965, 1966*

*Printed by Spottiswoode, Ballantyne & Co. Ltd
Bound by the Leighton-Straker Bookbinding Co. Ltd*

# CONTENTS

| | PAGE |
|---|---|
| The Golden Duck | 1 |
| The Tailor and the Hunter | 14 |
| Sambar the Mouse | 24 |
| The Millet Thief | 35 |
| The Hazel Twig | 40 |
| The Enchanted Princess | 49 |
| The Table, the Donkey and the Cudgel | 56 |
| The Tale of the Hard Heart | 65 |
| The Three Dogs | 77 |
| The Snake King | 87 |
| The Three Musicians | 97 |
| The Nine Hills of Rambin | 108 |
| The Cobbler's Two Sons | 122 |
| The Three White Doves | 131 |
| The Shepherd Boy's Dream | 141 |
| Little Earthworm | 151 |
| The Wolf and the Nightingale | 161 |
| The Christmas Present | 174 |

# I

# The Golden Duck

DEEP in the forests of Königgratz there stands a tiny cottage in which strange and wonderful things once happened many, many years ago. There lived a widow woman, Mrs. Jutta, with her daughter Adelheid, and the two orphan children of her dead brother, Heinrich and Emma. They were good, nice children, and all three did all they could to help their mother and aunt.

One evening there was a dreadful thunderstorm and they all sat crouched together listening to the drumming of the rain and watching the brilliant flashes of lightning, while the thunder rolled and rumbled terrifyingly about the mountains. Mrs. Jutta was telling them stories to keep them quiet, when, as she paused in her tale, there was a loud knock on the door and they all jumped. At first no one wanted to answer, but then Mrs. Jutta went to the door and asked who was there. A woman's soft voice answered: she was a traveller, she said, overtaken in the forest by the night and the storm, and hoping that she had come to a hospitable place.

Mrs. Jutta opened the door, and all their fears vanished when they saw an elderly woman with a noble face, who then stepped into the little room. She looked both nice and kind, and in a few minutes the children were vying with each other to do what they could for her, but all she would accept was a bowl of milk. By this time the storm was over and they all lay down to sleep.

In the morning, when Mrs. Jutta and the children woke, they were astounded to see not the old woman of the previous evening, but a woman of supernatural beauty, who wore a gown of white silk and across her glorious hair a scarf that sparkled with diamonds and other precious stones so brightly that they were almost dazzled. Turning to Mrs. Jutta, the stranger said:

"You must know that it is no mortal you have sheltered. I am the fairy Silenia, and it is my custom first to test those I intend to favour, in order to be sure that they are worthy. I have found you worthy, and above all I wish to reward sweet little Emma, so to her I give the gift that whenever she weeps whether from sorrow or from joy, instead of tears, pearls shall fall from her eyes, and that the combings of her hair shall turn into threads of gold. But—you must be careful to see that fresh air never touches her face, else she will lose this miraculous gift and undergo a sad transformation. Therefore you must cover her sweet head with a veil before she goes out, and do not allow her to raise it till she is safely back indoors."

The strange and lovely woman stopped speaking and as they began to thank her, she vanished. Mrs. Jutta felt that she must at once put the fairy's words to the test, so she sat little Emma on a sheet and began to comb her long golden hair. And, wonder of wonders, the hairs that fell on to the sheet turned at once into threads of gold. Then, when Mrs. Jutta explained to the children how they would now soon be rich and able to buy the loveliest toys, little Emma began to weep for joy and the loveliest little pearls rolled down her cheeks on to the sheet.

The next day Mrs. Jutta went to the town and sold the gold threads and the pearls and with the money bought a lovely veil. After that Emma was never allowed to leave the house without this on her head.

From that time on Mrs. Jutta used to comb Emma's hair several times a day, and she told her the loveliest stories that made her weep tears of delight and of sadness. In this way Mrs. Jutta soon had a considerable store of gold and pearls. At first she sold to the shops in the town, but they knew her as a poor woman and suspected her of having stolen the gold and pearls, or of having found them, and they gave her a very bad price indeed; but then she began selling to itinerant goldsmiths and jewellers and they paid her the full value, so that in no time she was able to buy a fine house and they had lovely clothes and everything they wanted.

The years passed and Adelheid and Emma grew up. Emma was lovely and clever and sweet. That, however, did not prevent their neighbours from being jealous, and some wicked tongues began spreading horrible rumours about the source of Mrs. Jutta's prosperity, while some even went so far as to say that she was a witch. Because of this, Mrs. Jutta decided that she would sell the house and go and live in the city that was the capital of that country. First, however, she decided to send Heinrich to look for a suitable house for them there.

Heinrich came to the city and there, being a good-looking young man with perfect manners and lots of money and intelligence, everyone thought him the young son of a knight, or even of a prince, who had adopted a humble name for some private reason, and thus he made the acquaintance of several young counts and nobles. He became great friends with Count Wenzel of Hasenburg and before long he knew all the Count's secrets. One evening when they were together as usual, Heinrich, though his aunt had warned him never to mention his sister or the source of his riches, was incautious enough to tell his friend all about her. He painted her beauty and sweetness so graphically that Count Wenzel fell in love with her on the spot and told Heinrich that he wanted to marry her. He explained that he was not interested in the miraculous way her hair turned to gold and her tears to pearls, for he himself owned so much land that he had more money than he knew what to do with. It was her sweetness and her loveliness he wanted, and he did not mind how humble her birth was.

So the Count wrote a letter to Emma and gave it to Heinrich who rode off home to deliver it to his sister, rather afraid of what his aunt would say to him for having told the Count his sister's secret. The idea of her niece becoming a rich young Countess appealed greatly to Mrs. Jutta, however, and Heinrich was so loud and sincere in his praises of his friend that in the end Emma agreed that she would marry him. Heinrich then rode back to the city where he gave his friend the good news, and Count Wenzel at once had a coach prepared so that Emma could travel in it without the air touching her face, and he sent this to bring her to his castle of Hasenburg.

So, in due course, Emma set out in the Count's coach

## THE GOLDEN DUCK

accompanied by Mrs. Jutta and Adelheid. They had covered almost half the distance and were travelling through a forest. It was a very hot day, so oppressive that Emma had lifted her veil. All at once, as Emma sat there with her face uncovered, something occurred to Mrs. Jutta that she wished to say to the young squire the Count had sent with the coach to escort his bride, and incautiously she opened the door of the carriage. In streamed the fresh air and sunlight, and no sooner had the sunbeams touched Emma's lovely young face than she turned into a golden duck which flew off and had soon vanished from the sight of her astounded aunt.

When Mrs. Jutta recovered her senses, she felt horribly afraid of the anger of so young and powerful a person as Count Wenzel and of Heinrich too. Then, when she realized that the Count's squire had not noticed what had happened, a wicked idea came into her head and she decided to put it into practice.

A little further on, they saw a village ahead and Mrs. Jutta stopped the coach and asked the squire to get her a drink of milk, and when he had gone, she put Emma's veil on her own daughter, Adelheid. When the squire returned, he found Mrs. Jutta outside the coach screaming and lamenting and with tears pouring down her cheeks. She told the young man that while he had been gone, she and Adelheid had taken a short stroll in order to get some air; when they were only a short distance from the coach some armed men had burst out from among the trees, seized her daughter and carried her off. She begged the squire to pursue them and try to rescue her daughter. She seemed so upset and her grief so genuine, that it never occurred to the squire that her story might not be true, and he was so sorry for her that he searched almost the whole forest. Naturally, he never found a trace of anyone. Meanwhile Mrs. Jutta told Adelheid that she must pretend to be Emma and marry the Count instead, and the poor girl agreed.

After this the squire did not dare leave the coach for a moment. When they stopped for the night, Mrs. Jutta gave Adelheid further instruction in how to behave like Emma, and gave her a great store of pearls and gold thread and showed her how she could use them to dupe the young Count. She also begged the squire to take them straight to Hasenburg and not first to the capital as had been intended. In this way she hoped to avoid meeting Heinrich, at least for some time.

When they reached Hasenburg, Mrs. Jutta got out of the coach first and told the Count that she and her niece must have a room into which no daylight came. There, she said, Emma must stay till she had recovered from the journey, for her wonderful gift had made her very sensitive. Meanwhile, she must receive no visits, not even from her betrothed. Eager though the Count was for his first glimpse of Heinrich's sister, he could only agree to what Mrs. Jutta asked. A suite of the finest rooms was put at the ladies' disposal, and the middle one of these was shrouded in darkness. To this Mrs. Jutta led her veiled daughter, and there hid for several days.

Meanwhile Heinrich, having heard that they had reached Hasenburg, had ridden from the capital to see his sister; but when he got there his aunt made the same excuses as to the Count and after a day or two Heinrich rode back to the city.

The Count was so sorry for Mrs. Jutta because she

had lost her own daughter, that he was most considerate and patient, and though each day he was sent sweet messages and little threads of gold and a few pearls, he finally lost patience and burst unannounced into the room where was the girl he thought to be Heinrich's sister. The pretended Emma at once flung her arms round his neck and kissed him most tenderly.

Mrs. Jutta reproached him for his impatience and hasty action and told him that because he had been unable to wait Emma could never recover all her beauty. The Count, of course, realized at once that Emma was nothing like the picture Heinrich had painted of her, but having given his word, he was quite prepared to marry her. So he sent for the castle chaplain and the ceremony was performed. It was not long before Count Wenzel realized that his wife was neither clever nor had a very sweet nature, as he had been led to expect. He was furious with Heinrich and went to the city to meet him, and there accused him of deceiving him, saying that his sister had neither beauty, intelligence nor sweetness, in fact none of the things Heinrich had said but the pearls and the golden threads in which he was not interested.

Heinrich was furious when he heard Count Wenzel say such things of his sister, whom he knew to be the loveliest girl in the whole country, and he told the Count that he must be mad, and then they both lost their tempers, and the Count had his servants take Heinrich prisoner and bring him to his castle, where he was thrown into the deepest dungeon.

At Hasenburg Castle there is still to be seen a tall round tower. To this a subterranean passage leads from the castle, but otherwise it has no way in or out except at the top, which is unroofed so that even the weather can persecute the prisoners in it. At the spot where the tower rests on the rock is a single barred window. It was into this tower that innocent Heinrich was cast, and Mrs. Jutta could only be glad, as it saved her from discovery, which would have been inevitable if Heinrich had seen Adelheid posing as his sister.

The poor Count thought that he had been the victim of a plot, so he condemned Heinrich to spend his life in the tower, and from then on treated his wife with the greatest indifference and contempt, often not even seeing her for weeks and months on end. Adelheid suffered pangs of conscience for what she had done and that, together with the burden of her husband's contempt, finally made her ill.

Meanwhile, Heinrich sat despairing in the tower with no hope of ever getting out. One night as he lay wondering whether it would not be better if he were dead, he heard a voice singing a song that he knew. And he knew the voice too; it was his sister's. Looking up, he saw in the bright moonlight a duck anxiously flying round and round. Its feathers seemed made of gold and there were pearls round its neck. Still Heinrich could not understand where his sister's voice had come from. Then the duck said: "Do you not know me? Has your unhappy sister become a stranger?"

Then Heinrich said: "I recognize your voice, but how do you come to be in this form?"

Then Emma told her brother all that had happened on the journey, and how their aunt had passed Adelheid off as the Count's bride. Poor Emma wept over her fate and that of her poor brother, and her tears rolled as pearls to the bottom of the tower. Brother

# THE GOLDEN DUCK

"Do you not know me?" said the duck. "Has your unhappy sister become a stranger?"

and sister comforted each other as best they could, but Heinrich was full of remorse, for it was his indiscretion in telling Count Wenzel about his sister that had led to their misfortunes. When day came, the duck flew away, promising to return that night.

Night after night Heinrich received a visit from the golden duck, and brother and sister did what they could to comfort each other. Heinrich even began to hope that he might have a chance of speaking to the Count and telling him all that had happened. After a while, however, the duck stopped coming, and Heinrich could only think that it had been caught because of its golden plumage or even killed. Then, for the first time since his imprisonment, he heard the bolts and bars of the double iron door to his prison being drawn, and in came the Captain of the Guard who told him that he was free and conducted him to the apartments that had been his in happier times. Heinrich asked the reason for this sudden change, but no one could tell him. Then the Count entered the room, took him by the hand and most earnestly begged his forgiveness. Then the Count told Heinrich how the guards had reported the visits of the golden duck to the tower and how it and the prisoner talked together, and how he, the Count, had gone one night and listened at the barred window and so he now knew everything and that Heinrich had had nothing to do with the wicked deception that had been practised upon him. He also told him how, determined to possess the duck, he had summoned all his fowlers and they had in fact caught it, but as they were putting it into the cage that had been prepared for it, it had got free and flown away. He told Heinrich that as he could not have Emma as his wife, he would give anything to have the golden duck live in his castle and he hoped that Heinrich would help him to persuade her to do so.

Heinrich forgave the Count for what he had done to him and promised to try and persuade the duck to stay, if it should come to visit him again. Meanwhile Adelheid had been growing weaker and weaker and now she died. The Count thereupon banished her mother to an ancient fortress right on the very fringe of his possessions and forbade her ever to appear before his eyes again, and thus punished her for what she had done.

For a long time Heinrich and the Count waited in vain for the duck to pay another visit to the castle. Finally, one evening when Heinrich sat on alone at the dining-table which the Count had left, the duck flew in through the open window and began eating crumbs off the table. The duck complained bitterly of the Count's attempts to catch and cage her, so Heinrich decided that he would not tell the Count of his sister's new visit. The Count, however, saw her as she flew out of the window again, and when Heinrich said nothing to him of the visit, his old suspicions revived. The next day the duck visited Heinrich in his room. No sooner had she flown in, than the window shut seemingly of its own accord, though in reality the Count had pulled it to with a string, and a few minutes later the Count himself came in to make sure of his prize. The duck was too quick, however, and escaped through the key-hole. The Count and Heinrich bitterly reproached each other and they parted in anger.

Heinrich now felt sure that he was never going to see his sister again, and he decided that he would leave the castle and seek his fortune in the wide world. As he walked along and was in the middle of a wood of dense firs, he saw a woman standing in his path and recognized the fairy Silenia.

"Why have you left Hasenburg," said the fairy, her noble face grave and almost threatening, "just as the evil fate that your carelessness brought upon your sister was about to change for the better? Go back at once. You will find the Count in a state that will lead to happiness, encourage him in it and soon Emma will be with you again. Go!"

With those words the fairy disappeared, and Heinrich turned and retraced his steps. He had not gone far, before he met several of the Count's men who had been sent to find him and to beg him to return, because the Count was sick with remorse and loneliness. So Heinrich rode back to Hasenburg with them, and there he found that the Count was indeed ill and in bed. When Heinrich entered his room the Count greeted him lovingly, and when Heinrich had told him what the fairy had said, the Count swore that he would remain ever faithful to the memory of Emma, his true love and bride. Scarcely had he spoken the words than the window opened and the golden duck flew in, settled on the bedpost and said:

"This is the last time I shall appear to you in this form, for my time of testing is over and I am to be allowed to find life anew in the arms of my dear husband."

At that the golden feathers began to flutter from the duck's body, its long beak became round and soon had turned into a chin topped by a lovely little red mouth, above which appeared two rosy cheeks and a pair of sparkling dark eyes. Before they realized it, there stood a lovely maiden clad in a rich gown of cloth of gold embroidered with pearls and precious stones.

At the sight of her the Count felt quite cured of all his sorrows; he leapt from his bed and knelt at the feet of his lovely bride. A few days later they were married and it was one of the most splendid and magnificent weddings that had ever been seen in the land.

## II

# The Tailor and the Hunter

ONCE there was a tailor who grew tired of being a tailor and set off into the world in search of adventure. He walked on and on, and at the end of the first day he reached a dark and gloomy forest and plunged into it. After a while he heard someone singing. Going closer, he saw a hunter sitting at the foot of a tree, singing a song. The tailor asked him why he was sitting in the forest singing instead of hunting. "I'm tired of just hunting," said the hunter, "I want something more exciting. I want adventure." Delighted at finding, as he thought, a kindred spirit, the tailor suggested that he and the hunter go along together. The hunter agreed, and they set off. Darkness fell and they were still in the forest, so they decided to spend the night there. They both climbed into a tall tree and slept soundly.

When they awoke, it was daybreak and they walked on again. They walked for a long time, talking together all the while, and then suddenly they heard somebody laugh very loudly. Looking up they saw a little man who beckoned to them with his finger. They followed him and soon found themselves in front of a big castle. The little man knocked on the great iron gate with his little stick and the gate opened. Then the little man

## THE TAILOR AND THE HUNTER

pointed to a door across the courtyard and vanished. Thinking that this meant that they were to go through that door, the tailor took the hunter by the hand and in they walked. They found themselves in a kitchen with a small fireplace on the left and on the right another door. This door led into a big room with two beds, a table and two chairs. It all looked as though it had been prepared specially for them.

The hunter was bold and brave, but not the tailor. He was more cautious than brave and suggested that it would be best if only one went to bed, while the other kept watch. They could take it in turn.

The first night the tailor kept watch. He drew up a stool to the hearth in the kitchen, for it was late in the autumn and cold at night. The hunter lay down in one of the beds in the other room and by the time midnight approached, he was sound asleep.

At midnight the door into the kitchen slowly opened and in came a dwarf, dressed in green. He went to the fireplace, held his hands out to the warmth and gave the tailor a pitiful look. Seeing this, the tailor put another log on the fire, hoping that that would please the little man, and, indeed, it seemed to be what he wanted, for he patted the tailor's shoulder and then left looking quite cheerful.

At daybreak the hunter awoke, and as he sat up in bed to call to the tailor he saw on the table a number of dishes. He jumped out of bed and fetched the tailor and the two hungry men sat down to what was a delicious meal.

That night it was the hunter's turn to keep watch. Rather frightened, the tailor went to bed, while the brave hunter made up a big fire in the hearth and settled himself in the kitchen. Again the little man appeared at midnight and went up to the fire, but this time it was not the kindly tailor there. The hunter, a rough, inconsiderate man, did not like such a small little person daring to come up to his fire, and so he took a stick and struck the dwarf's fingers a smart blow when he stretched out his hands to the fire. The dwarf was furious at the hunter's hard-heartedness and lack of manners and walked away, saying, "You will regret this!" in a threatening tone.

The tailor had said nothing to the hunter about the visit he had received from the little dwarf, thinking he would wait to see if the hunter received one too. Now, when the hunter told him what had happened, the tailor told his story and reproached the hunter for having been so unkind and rude.

That evening it was the tailor's turn to keep watch again. Now he was much more afraid than he had been before. At midnight, just as before, the little dwarf appeared and came up to the fire to warm himself. Wishing to make up for the hunter's bad behaviour, the tailor put several logs on the fire, not just one. The little dwarf was very pleased, and taking a ring from his finger, put it on one of the tailor's fingers, saying: "If there is any wish you want fulfilled, you have only to turn this ring on your finger and immediately I shall be there and at your service." Then the dwarf bowed rather formally and vanished.

In the morning, the tailor told the hunter of the dwarf's visit, but he said nothing about the ring. The hunter laughed at the tailor for being nice to the dwarf and said: "Just you wait and see; I'll soon get rid of the little chap." The tailor warned him not to try, for he was sure that the castle they were in belonged to the dwarf, and that if they were rude or behaved badly they would regret it. The hunter would not listen to him, so the tailor tried to persuade him to come away. The hunter, however, wanted to give the poor dwarf a real thrashing so that he would keep away from the kitchen for good.

That night the hunter went to keep watch, while the tailor got into bed, where he lay shivering and shaking, too frightened at the thought of what might happen to be able to get to sleep. At the same hour of midnight the dwarf appeared and came to the fire. As he held out his hands, the hunter began hitting him on the back as hard as he could. The dwarf was not patient and long-suffering, as he had been when the hunter struck his fingers; now he called out in a loud voice and in an instant the kitchen was swarming with little dwarfs who fell upon the hunter and gave him a thorough, sound thrashing, forcing him to run to the door and rush out into the night to escape. The tailor had jumped out of bed when he heard the commotion and he too reached the open, though without receiving a blow.

The hunter and tailor ran for quite a distance, before they dare stop to recover their breath. The hunter felt sore all over, but he could not help laughing at the tailor who had been in such a hurry that he had forgotten to put on his clothes and was wearing just his shirt and socks. The tailor suddenly remembered his magic ring. He turned it on his finger and the next moment there were two dwarfs standing in front of him with his clothes. The tailor put them on and immediately the dwarfs vanished.

The hunter was speechless with astonishment. He

felt sure that the tailor had made a secret pact with the dwarfs and felt very suspicious of him. In fact, he would have liked to have got rid of him.

The hunter and the tailor ran for

They walked on, and after a long while they came to a tree and sat down for a rest. They felt very hungry and longed for food. Again the tailor remembered his ring, turned it and immediately the ground opened at their very feet in a great yawning gulf. Out of this gulf appeared four dwarfs carrying a table which they placed between the two men. Then out came seven dwarfs carrying dishes and they were followed by

quite a distance before they dare stop.

five more dwarfs with plates and knives and forks and spoons and chairs, and bottles of wine too. When everything was in its place, the dwarfs vanished.

This time the hunter was too hungry to feel surprised. He fell upon the food and ate and ate, never stopping to wonder at the way the food had got there. When both had eaten as much as they wanted, the table and all the other things just vanished.

Only now did it occur to the hunter that the food and dishes and all the rest of it had been brought by dwarfs and he remembered how, before, the tailor had had his clothes brought him by two dwarfs. He was sure now that the tailor was in league with the dwarfs, and he became more suspicious of him than ever.

The kindly tailor noticed nothing. It was a strange thing, but ever since he had had the magic ring on his finger he had never once felt afraid. In fact, now, he was even braver than the hunter.

At last they came out of the forest and reached a highroad that led them on and on and eventually brought them to a city. They entered the city and soon they noticed how sad everyone looked. When they asked why everybody was so sad, they were told that the city was ruled by a very hard-hearted king. The king's daughter was about to be married, and the king had ordered that in turn all the tailors of the city were to make his daughter a gown until she had one that the king thought fine and becoming enough; the tailor who made that gown would get a handsome reward; those whose gowns were rejected must prepare to die.

The tailor thought that he ought to try to help, so he sought out the house of a tailor. This happened to be the one who was to make the first gown. The gown was to be taken to the king the following morning, and the man and his family were in the depths of despair, for they all felt that he would never come home again. The tailor felt very sorry for him and promised to save him. He asked for the material, which had already been cut out, and took it with him into the room that had been set aside for him and his companion, the hunter. The tailor turned the ring on his finger and, as he did so, wished that the dwarfs would finish the gown while everyone was asleep. Then he got into bed and went fast asleep. At midnight, however, he woke to find two dwarfs standing beside his bed and they handed him the gown, all ready and finished.

In the morning the tailor gave the gown to the other tailor who took it in fear and trembling to the king. The princess put it on and it fitted perfectly. No one in the world could have made it better. The tailor was given the promised reward and ran home delightedly, only to find that his two helpers had already left to continue their journey.

The tailor, was very pleased at having been able to help the poor man and make him happy, thereby, perhaps, saving a number of people from death. But the hunter was now very jealous indeed of the tailor.

They walked on and on for a long way, and finally they came to a lonely meadow in the middle of which they saw an enormous stone. They walked across and examined the stone. There seemed to be something queer about it, and they tried to shift it, but it was far too heavy even for the two of them to move. So the tailor turned his ring and instantly the stone rolled away from its position, exposing a great hole in the ground. They were both very curious to know what was inside there, at the bottom, and they decided to investigate. The hunter made ropes of straw, fastened them together till they were strong enough to bear the tailor's weight and lowered him down.

The tailor thought that he had come into a different world. Never had he seen such beauty as there was down there. He went through a lovely garden and so came to a castle. As he stood gazing at it in wonderment, three princesses came out. They were sisters, they told the tailor, and had been carried off by a dragon and brought to this castle, so that their parents and friends did not know where they were. The dragon used to fly away somewhere every day, but when it came back the princesses had to bring its food, which it ate in the garden. After that it would lie down with its head on their laps and they had to stroke it while it slept. The princesses' father had promised that whoever should find and free his daughters should have his kingdom and marry the youngest of the princesses.

The three princesses begged the tailor to save them. This meant that he would have to fight the dragon, but the tailor was quite ready to do that. The princesses gave him a sword and told him to hide behind some bushes and wait till the dragon arrived. Meanwhile the princesses sat down on a grassy bank.

Before very long the tailor heard a roaring and looking up saw flames darting up into the air. Then, snorting mightily, the dragon came into the garden, and after it had had its meal, lay down with its head on the princesses' laps. The princesses began to stroke the dragon, and soon it fell asleep.

Then the tailor came out from behind the bush and thrust his sword into the dragon's neck, killing it and so rescuing the princesses. Quickly the tailor and the three princesses hurried to the bottom of the great hole and called to the hunter, who had been wondering what on earth the tailor had been doing. One by one the hunter pulled the princesses up, but when it was the tailor's turn and the tailor was half-way up, the hunter cut the rope. The poor tailor fell back to the bottom and there he stayed, quite forgetting his ring.

Meanwhile the hunter went with the three princesses to the king and told him such a story that the king thought that it was the hunter who had rescued his daughters. The king kept his word and arranged for the youngest princess to marry the hunter.

Then, when the wedding day was at hand, the tailor at last remembered his ring. He turned it, and in a moment hundreds of dwarfs were busy building a long flight of stairs to get him out of the great hole. When it was ready, the tailor walked up and emerged at the top. Here he again turned his ring and wished that a dwarf might show him the way to the king's palace. At once a dwarf appeared and took him before the king.

The tailor then told the king that it was really he who had rescued the princesses, and when the king asked the princesses if that were so, they said that it was, indeed.

Because the hunter had helped them out of the hole, the king gave him a casket of gold, but banished him from the kingdom for ever, while to the tailor he gave his kingdom and his youngest daughter. They were married and lived happily, ruling their subjects wisely and well, but whether they are still alive I do not know.

## III

# Sambar the Mouse

DEEP within a large and lonely wood in a far part of the country stood a huge, immensely tall tree with many boughs and branches. In this tree a raven had its nest.

One day, when the raven was sitting in its tree, it saw a bird-catcher come and spread his net under the tree. The raven was frightened and said to itself: "I wonder if this bird-catcher has set his net for me or for others? I must stay here and see."

The bird-catcher, an old man, sprinkled grain on the ground to act as bait, stretched his line and hid in the bushes to wait. Soon a pigeon came flying along with a flock of other pigeons of which it was the leader. It saw the grain and flew down to feed, paying no attention to the line. As the pigeons settled, the net closed over them and they were caught. The bird-catcher was delighted, but the pigeons fluttered their wings in panic. Then the pigeon who was the leader of the flock, said:

"Let no one think of just himself. We must all help each other. If we all take off together, then perhaps we shall be able to raise the net and take it with us."

That is what the pigeons did. They took off all at the same time, and they did in fact succeed in raising the net and flying off with it. The old bird-catcher watched them go and then began to run after them, so as to mark the place where they would alight. The raven in the great tree said to itself: "I must follow them and see how this is going to end."

When the leader of the pigeons saw that the bird-catcher was following the line of their flight, it said to the others:

"Look, the bird-catcher is following us; if we fly straight, he will always keep sight of us and we shall never escape. So let us fly across hills and valleys; if we do that he is bound to lose sight of us and will have to give up following us. Not far from here is a ravine, where a mouse lives, who is a friend of mine. I know that he will gnaw through the net and free us, if we fly there."

The pigeons followed the advice of their leader, and that is how the bird-catcher lost sight of them. The raven, however, flew along slowly behind them, for it wanted to see what the end of the matter would be, and how the pigeons would get themselves out of the net.

Then the pigeons reached the ravine where the mouse lived. There they alighted and saw that the mouse had at least a hundred entrances and exits to its underground dwelling, so that it always had a way of escape if danger threatened. The name of that mouse was Sambar. The leader of the pigeons then called to his friend:

"Sambar, come out!"

"Who are you?" the mouse called back.

"It is I, the pigeon, your friend."

Then the mouse came and peered cautiously out of

one of its innumerable holes. When it saw the pigeon, it said:

"My dear pigeon, what has been happening to you?"

Then the pigeon said:

"My dear mouse, Fate plays evil tricks on everybody. For us it strewed some most tempting grains of wheat on the ground and blinded my eyes so that I never saw the net, with the result that I and my friends were caught in it. No one can do anything against Providence that comes from above. After all, the sun and moon suffer eclipse, and man even lures fish out of the depths of the sea, catching them in treacherous nets as he does the birds of the air."

When the pigeon had finished this rather eloquent speech, the mouse began gnawing the net, starting at the end where its friend, the leader of the pigeons, stood. The pigeon then said:

"Start with one of the others, and when all are free, then let me out."

The mouse, however, paid no attention to this, but just went on gnawing at the net. Again the pigeon asked it to start with one of the others, and then the mouse said:

"Why do you keep asking me to start with one of the others, as if you did not want to be free too?"

Then the pigeon answered:

"Please do not be offended at my insistence, but these my companions trusted to me as their leader; they followed me gladly and with utter confidence and through lack of circumspection got caught in the net; therefore it is only right that I should see to their release before thinking of my own, especially as it was only by their joint effort that we were able to take off with the net. Also, suppose you were to tire, you might perhaps feel unable to go on gnawing; but if you know that I, your dearest friend, am still in the net, you will never forsake me."

Then Sambar the Mouse said:

"My dear, good Pigeon! That sentiment does you great honour and must only strengthen the love between you and your companions."

So the mouse gnawed away at the net, till all the pigeons were free and had flown happily away, then it scuttled back into its hole.

The raven had flown into a nearby tree, from where it had seen and heard everything. Now it communed with itself.

"Who knows," the raven said, "one day I may find myself in the same situation and in the same danger as those pigeons. And what a wonderful thing it is to have noble friends to help you in your need. I should like to make friends with this mouse."

So the raven flew from the tree onto the ground, hopped to the mouse-holes and called:

"Sambar, come out!"

The mouse replied from the inside:

"Who are you?"

"I am the raven," replied the other. "I have just seen what happened to your dear friend the pigeon and how he was rescued by your loyalty; and so I have come to ask for your friendship."

Then Sambar, the wise little mouse, replied without coming out of his underground dwelling:

"There can be no friendship between you and me. A wise person strives to achieve only what is possible, and those who seek to accomplish the impossible are fools. It would be like a ship sailing the land, or a coach driving across the sea. How can there be friendship between us, when I am your prey and you my hunter?"

Then said the raven:

"My dear mouse, you misunderstand me. You, alive, will be a help to me, your friendship as enduring as amber that smells sweetly even when you carry it hidden."

To that the mouse replied:

"You must know, Raven, that hatred engendered by desire is the greatest of all hates. Lions and elephants hate each other because of their strength. That is a noble and equal hatred of the brave vying with each other; but the inveterate hatred of the strong for the weak, that is an ignoble and unequal hatred; the hatred of the hawk for the partridge, of the cat for the rat, of the dog for the rabbit, of you—for me. You can heat water till it burns you like fire, but that will not make it fire, nor the friend of fire; indeed, hot water poured onto fire will put it out. The sage says: 'who associates with his enemy is like one who takes a poisonous snake in his hand; he never knows when it will bite him.' The wise man never trusts his enemy, but keeps away from him, otherwise the same will happen to him as happened to the man with the snake."

"What happened to him?" asked the raven.

Then the mouse told him the following tale:

A long time ago there was man in whose house there lived a snake. The man's wife used to look after this snake and feed it every day. The snake lived in a hole in the wall by the hearth, where it was always nice and warm. The man and his wife, being superstitious, thought that it brought luck to have a snake in the house. Now, one Sunday the man had a headache and so he stayed in bed, letting his wife and the servants go to church alone. When they were all gone and the house was quite still, the snake slipped out of its hole and looked round cautiously. The man saw the snake through the open door of his room and wondered why it looked round so carefully, which he had never seen it do before. As he watched, the snake crawled round and inspected all the corners of the room; it even came into the man's bedroom, but saw no one, for the man had kept himself hidden. Then the snake crawled to the hearth where a pot of soup hung over the fire, poked its head over the rim of the pot and spat its venom into the soup. Then the snake went and hid again. The man got up, went to the kitchen, took the pot and buried it in the ground, soup and all.

Dinner-time came, which was when the snake usually came out for its food, and the man took up position beside the hole holding an axe with which he intended to chop the snake's head off. But the snake was cautious and only stuck its head out a tiny way, and, as the man struck, drew it back like lightning, all of which showed that it did not have a clear conscience. After some days the woman tried to persuade her husband that he should make peace with the snake, for she was sure that it would never do anything wicked again. The man agreed and called a neighbour to be witness of the agreement with the snake and to draw up a pact between them, so that the two could feel sure of the other. They then called the snake and made the proposal. The snake, however, said:

"No. We can never be friends again. When you think what I put in your pot, and when I think how you struck at my head with your sharp axe, neither will feel able to trust the other. Give me passage and let me go my way, that is all I ask of you. The further from you I am, the better. You must stay in your house." And so it was.

After listening to this long tale, the raven said:

"I see the point of your tale. I would, however, ask you to consider your nature and my honesty, and not to be so severe and refuse me your friendship. There is a difference between the noble and the ignoble: a beaker made of gold lasts longer than one of glass; if the glass one breaks, it is worthless, but if a golden beaker is dented it does not lose its value. The friendship of those who are bad and ignoble is no friendship. You, however, have a noble character, as I have seen, and my heart desires your friendship and needs it, and I shall not move from the entrances to your dwelling, nor eat, nor drink, till you grant my request."

Then clever Mouse Sambar replied:

"Very well, I accept your friendship, for I have never refused a just request. But you must remember that I have not come begging to you, and that in my dwelling I am safe from you. So do not congratulate yourself on having found a careless and stupid mouse, or you may find yourself like the cock with the fox."

"What happened to the cock?" asked the raven, so then the mouse told him the following tale:

One cold winter's night a fox crept out of its earth and went hunting, for it was very, very hungry. As it was passing a farm, it heard a cock crowing and crowing. The cock was on the roof of the house and had been crowing all night. The fox slunk up to the house and said to the cock:

"Mr. Cock, why are you singing on this cold, dark night?"

The cock replied:

"I am announcing the day that my nature tells me is coming."

"Mr. Cock," the fox went on, "if you know what is going to happen before it happens, then you have an element of the divine in you."

Having said that the fox began to dance.

Then the cock asked:

"Mr. Fox, why do you dance?"

"When you sing, Wise Master," replied the fox, "it is only right that I dance, for it is but fitting to dance when people are gay. O Cock, noble prince of all birds, you are not only talented in that you can fly through the air, but Nature has even given you the great gift of prophecy. Oh, how favoured you are among all creatures. How happy I would be if you would grant me your favour, if I might be allowed to kiss your wise and noble head. Oh, how my friends would envy me, if I could tell them that I was the fortunate one to whom the prophet had bent his head so that I might kiss it!"

The stupid cock believed the flattery of the cunning fox, flew down from the tree and held out its head to be kissed. The fox bit it off with one snap of his jaws and, laughing, said:

"I have found this prophet bereft of all reason."

When he had finished this little tale, the mouse continued, speaking now to the raven:

"I have not told you that tale because I think that I

am the cock and you the fox, I the food and you the one who will eat me; I much prefer to believe that you do not speak with the forked tongue of the serpent." The mouse then turned and went into one of the entrances to his underground dwelling.

Seeing that, the raven asked:

"Why do you go into your doorway? What makes you so shy of coming out to me? Are you still afraid of me?" The mouse then replied:

"I have put my faith and reliance in you, because I like you. Nor is it fear that you might be dishonest that keeps me from coming out. But you have many companions of your kind, though perhaps not of your way of thinking, and their friendship I do not trust. If one of them should see me, then I would be afraid of his eating me."

The raven said:

"The essence of true friendship is that one is a faithful friend of one's companions and the enemy of his enemies; rest assured, my dear Sambar, that I have no friend who will not be as true a friend to you, as I myself. And I have power and strength enough to protect and defend you."

Then, at last, the Mouse Sambar came out of its hole and swore everlasting friendship with the raven. When they had done that, they lived together in peace and friendship, and every day they told each other beautiful and entertaining tales.

One day the raven said to the mouse:

"Listen, dear Sambar, your home is too near the road, I am afraid someone may come along and kill you or me; also I am finding it difficult to find food here. But I know of a better and pleasanter place to

Then at last the Mouse Sambar came out of its hole.

stay in, where there is water and meadowland, fruit and food for us both, and in the lake there lives an old friend of mine, a true friend; I wish you would move there with me."

"For your sake I will go," replied Sambar, the mouse. "Being a shy and retiring person, I do not feel altogether safe here, that is why, as you see, I have so many entrances and exits to my dwelling. Believe me, dear friend, I have in my life encountered many dangers, of which I shall tell you when we get to this new place."

After that the two said farewell to the ravine and all that was in it; the raven took the mouse by its little tail and flew with it to the place of which he had spoken. There an animal poked its head out of the water, but took fright when it saw the mouse, which it did not know. As the raven released its hold of the mouse's tail, the creature dived again quickly and disappeared. The raven flew up into a tree and called "Corax, Corax," and at that the animal came out of the water. It was the raven's great friend, the turtle. The turtle was delighted to see the raven again and asked the reason why he had stayed away so long. Then the raven told the turtle about the pigeon and the mouse and introduced his two friends. The turtle was most impressed by the great intelligence of the mouse, crawled up and gave Sambar its hand, assuring him how pleased it was to make his acquaintance.

And there the three friends lived peacefully together for the rest of their lives.

## IV

# The Millet Thief

IN a town—it does not matter where and it does not matter when—there once lived a very rich merchant in a very large house which had behind it a big and magnificent garden, in which there was a plot sown with millet. One day, in the late springtime, when the rich merchant went for a stroll round his garden, to his great annoyance and anger he saw that in the night some of his millet, which was already standing fresh and strong, had been cropped or torn up by some bold and thieving hand. He was especially fond of just that corner of his garden where he always grew his millet, so he made up his mind that he was going to catch the thief and punish him most severely or else hand him over to the police for damaging his crops. First, however, he called his three sons, Michael, George and John, and told them what had happened and what he intended to do.

"Last night," he said, "there was a thief in our garden. He cropped part of my young millet and I am very annoyed indeed. This trespasser must be caught whatever happens, and so you, my sons, must keep watch at night—one after another in turn. The one who catches the thief shall receive a large reward."

The eldest son, Michael, kept watch that first night.

He took several loaded pistols, a sharp sword, some food and something to drink, wrapped himself in a big warm cloak and settled himself under a bush of flowering elder to watch. But the Spring night air was warm and still and soon Michael felt drowsy and before he realized it he had fallen asleep, and when he woke up in the morning, he saw to his horror that a still larger piece of the young millet had been cropped. After that he had to admit to his father that he had been very tired and had fallen asleep. That made his father more angry than ever, and he scolded his eldest son and scornfully told him that he was a fine watcher and that he wished the thief had stolen him with his pistols and his sword instead of the millet.

Next night it was the turn of George, the merchant's second son. He was to keep watch. He took with him the same weapons as his brother Michael had had and also a stout cudgel and some strong rope. But the soft night air made this watcher feel sleepy too, and after several great yawns, he felt his eyelids growing heavier and heavier, and his head began to nod, and before he knew anything more, he was asleep too. In the morning he saw that the thief had been there again and had cropped still more of his father's millet. He was very ashamed and afraid to tell his father, and this time the merchant was really furious and said: "By the time the third brother has had his sleep, there will be no millet left and then we won't need a watcher any more."

The third night it was John's, the youngest, turn. Though his brothers did their best to persuade him, he took no weapons of any kind with him. Secretly he had found himself a well-tried way of keeping awake. He had collected a lot of thorny branches and thistles, and when he went to his hiding-place that evening he arranged them round so that if ever his head should nod, he would prick his nose and that would wake him up again at once. Thus John kept awake and as midnight approached he heard in the distance a clatter and a stamping. The sound came nearer and nearer, and then he could hear noises coming from the millet plot itself. "Ha," thought John, "now I'll get you. Where's the rope?" Then he pulled the rope out of his pocket, quietly moved the thorns aside and cautiously tiptoed towards the plot and the thief. When he came to the plot his eyes opened wide, for who would have thought it!—the thief was the sweetest and daintiest little pony in all the world. John was delighted with it, especially as it allowed itself to be caught and willingly followed him to the stable.

John now had plenty of time to go to his own bed and have a nice long sleep. In the morning, when his brothers got up and were about to go down and out into the garden, they saw to their astonishment that John was in bed sound asleep. They woke him and jeered at him and teased him, saying that he was the best watcher of them all, for he had not even been able to stay out all night at his post. They at least had done that. But John answered:

"You can keep your teasing to yourselves and come and see. Because I can show you the millet thief."

His father and brothers went with him, and he led them to the stables, where the strange and wonderful little pony stood gazing at them with large bright eyes. No one knew or was able to tell them where it had come from or whose it was. It was the most beautiful little mare, with slender legs and the colour of silver all over. The rich merchant was delighted and glad indeed, and he gave John the pony as his reward. John was very pleased with his present and called it "Thief".

Some time later the brothers heard that a beautiful princess who lived in the castle on the top of the Glass Mountain had been enchanted, but no one could get up there to take the spell from her, because the road was so slippery. However, if anyone could succeed in getting up there safely and then could ride three times round the castle, he, it was said, would save the Princess and have her for his bride. A number of young men had already attempted the dangerous ride up the mountain, but they had all fallen down the sheer mountain side and lay dead at the foot of it.

The news of these strange and dreadful doings spread throughout the country, and when the three brothers heard it, they all felt that they too would like to try their luck and see if they could not ride up the glass mountain and win the beautiful princess. Michael and George each bought himself a fine, strong young horse, and they had them well shod with shoes made with studs that would grip the slippery surface. John, of course, saddled his little mare, Thief, and so off they rode to try their luck.

Before long they came to the foot of the Glass Mountain. The eldest son was the first to try, but his horse slipped and both horse and rider, went tumbling to the foot of the mountain. Then George, the second brother, mounted and rode off, but his horse also slipped and fell and the two went toppling down the steep mountain side and lay quite still. Now it was John's turn. He mounted Thief, clicked his tongue and off they went. Clip, clop, clip, clop. Thief never stopped. Clip, clop, clip, clop, there they were at the top. Clip, clop, clip, clop, now they had ridden once round the castle. And again, clip, clop, clip, clop, till they had ridden three times round. It was just as though Thief had done it all hundreds of times before. Then Thief stopped at the castle door. It opened and a perfectly lovely princess came out towards them. She was dressed all in silk and gold, and joyfully she greeted the one who had freed her from the evil spell, her rescuer. Quickly John leaped from the saddle and hurried to embrace the princess and, with her all his great good fortune.

The Princess went to the mare and patted her: "Oh, you little rascal," she said. "Why did you run away from me? Without you I have not been able to spend the one hour of freedom I was allowed on the green earth! Now you must never dare leave us again."

Then at last John realized that his lovely Thief was a magic horse and really belonged to his princess, and he felt so proud and happy that these two lovely creatures were to be his very own for ever.

After a while John's two brothers recovered from their falls, but they never saw their young brother again, for he was living happily and freed of all earthly cares, with his wife, the princess, in her magic castle on the top of the Glass Mountain.

## V

# The Hazel Twig

ONCE there was a merchant whose business often sent him travelling in foreign countries. One day, as he was saying goodbye to his three daughters before setting off on one of these journeys, he said to them:

"My dears, when I come back I would like to bring you all some present to make you happy. Tell me honestly what you would like me to bring."

The eldest of the three daughters answered:

"Father, dear, please bring me a lovely pearl necklace."

The merchant's second daughter said:

"I should love to have a ring with a lovely big diamond."

But the youngest just gave her father a hug and whispered shyly:

"Just bring me a green hazel twig to show me that you have been thinking of me."

"All right, my dear daughters," said the merchant, "I will bring you the things you want." And so he set off on his journey.

This time his travels took him farther than ever, and he did good business. Nor did he forget the things his daughters had asked for. He bought an expensive pearl necklace and packed it in its case at the bottom of his big suitcase, and there too lay a tiny box with a valuable diamond ring for his second daughter. As he set out on the last stage of his journey home he began looking for a hazel bush to get the twig he had promised to bring his youngest daughter. He could see one nowhere. Whenever he entered a wood or forest, he would get out of his coach and walk, so as to be sure that he would not miss seeing a hazel bush if one was growing anywhere near the road. Yet, hard though he searched, there seemed to be no hazel bushes in that part of the world at all, and the poor merchant became very sad at the thought that he might not be able to fulfil the most modest of his three daughters' wishes.

Eventually he came to a dark and gloomy wood. Again the merchant alighted from his coach and walked along peering at the bushes on either side of the road. All at once his shoulder brushed against a twig and there was a rattling noise like the patter of hail-stones. The merchant looked at the twig and saw that it was a lovely green hazel twig with golden nuts hanging on it. How pleased and glad he was. He put out his hand and broke off the twig. At that very moment a savage bear burst out of the bushes nearby and rose up growling on its hind legs, looking as though it were just about to fall upon the poor merchant. In a deep, terrifying, growling voice the bear said:

"Why have you broken off my hazel twig? Why? I shall eat you up."

Trembling all over, the poor merchant said in a voice that shook with fear:

"Dear bear, please do not eat me and please let me

have this hazel twig to take home; for it I will give you a big ham and lots and lots of sausages."

But the bear growled in answer:

"Keep your ham and your sausages, but promise me this, that you will give me whatever first comes to meet you when you get home. If you promise me that, I will let you go."

The merchant agreed and promised, for he felt that his poodle would be sure to come running out when it heard the coach and thus be the first to greet him. Much though he loved his dog, he was prepared to sacrifice it to save his life. The bear held out his paws and shook the trembling merchant's hands as a sign that their bargain was made; then the bear turned and trotted back into the bushes. The merchant heaved a great sigh of relief, got into his coach and hastened home, the twig of golden hazels gleaming in his hat.

Soon the merchant came to his home. His family heard the coach and out came his youngest daughter, skipping gaily as she ran to welcome her father home. Behind her bounded the poodle, and the two other daughters and their mother came hurrying along behind. You can imagine how horrified the poor merchant was when he saw that his youngest daughter was the first to come to greet him. The more she hugged him and kissed him, the sadder he became. Hardly giving himself time to kiss the others, he told them what had happened when he plucked the hazel twig and of the awful promise he had had to make. They all burst into tears and it was a sad homecoming indeed.

Strangely enough the bravest, the one least afraid, was the youngest daughter, the one who was affected most. She said that of course the merchant must keep

## THE HAZEL TWIG

his promise: she was quite ready. But her mother thought and thought, and in the end she hit upon this way out:

"How," she said, "is the bear to know who came to meet you first? If the nasty thing really comes and wants to hold you to your promise, then instead of our dear girl here, we'll give him that little orphan girl who comes to work for us. He will be just as pleased, and he'll never know."

They all thought this a good idea, and soon they had recovered their spirits and were gay and happy, and delighted with the presents their father had brought back from his travels for them. The youngest daughter was happy with her hazel twig, and soon they had forgotten all about the bear and their father's promise.

One day, however, a large black coach drew up outside the merchant's gate and out stepped the great ugly bear. Growling mightily, the bear walked into the house and demanded that the frightened merchant fulfil his promise. With all speed and secrecy they got the orphan girl to come to the house, brushed her and combed her, gave her a fine dress to put on, and led her to the bear's coach. The poor girl, who was rather ugly, got in and the coach drove off.

The girl was surprised to find herself sitting beside a bear and not a little frightened when it laid its great shaggy head in her lap and growled:

> Scratch me, rub me,
>   Tickle my ears;
> Do it softly, do it well
> Or you'll never live the tale to tell.

Terrified, the girl began to scratch, and tickle behind the bear's ears. First the right, then the left, but she did not do it properly, and when the bear realized this, he knew that a trick had been played on him. He was so angry that he wanted to eat the terrified orphan girl, finery and all, but she managed to jump out of the coach and escaped.

Then the bear ordered his coachmen to turn, and he drove back to the merchant's house and, growling most menacingly, demanded that the merchant give him the right girl. So the merchant's poor youngest daughter had to go. Sorrowfully but bravely she said goodbye and got into the coach with the bear. The coach started, the bear laid his shaggy head in the girl's lap and growled again:

> Scratch me, rub me,
>   Tickle my ears;
> Do it softly, do it well
> Or you'll never live the tale to tell.

The merchant's daughter felt rather sorry for the bear. His coat was soft and warm and his shaggy head felt comfortable on her lap, so she scratched him behind the ears gently, yet firmly—and the bear loved it. A dreamy look came into his eye and the girl began to think him sweet and not horrid at all. The coach sped along; it tore through the forest like a mighty, rushing wind, and soon they came to the dark and gloomy wood where the merchant had first met the bear. All at once the coach stopped. They were outside the mouth of a cave. This was where the bear lived. When she saw the dark, gaping opening in the rock, the poor girl could not help feeling afraid. Then the bear put his great hairy arm round her shoulders and said in a friendly growl:

"Here you must live and be happy. Of course you will have to behave yourself, otherwise my wild creatures may tear you to pieces."

So they entered the gaping mouth of the cave and after a few steps, they came to a heavy iron door which the bear opened. They now found themselves in a room full of venomous snakes, all darting their tongues greedily at them. The bear growled softly to the girl:

> Look not around,
> Neither to left, nor right,
> Eyes on the ground
> And you will be all right.

So the girl walked through the room with her eyes fixed in front of her, never looking round or anywhere but straight at the ground in front of her. And not a snake moved. After this first room, there were ten other rooms through which they had to pass, all filled with horrid, terrifying creatures; and the last was worst of all, for it was full of dragons, snakes, bloated toads, basilisks and winged serpents. And as they entered each room, the bear growled his little jingle:

> Look not around,
> Neither to left, nor right,
> Eyes on the ground
> And you will be all right.

The poor girl, of course, was terrified, and trembled like an aspen leaf, but she walked on bravely and looked neither right nor left, and never turned her head. Then, as they set foot in the twelfth room, they saw a gleam of light ahead, sweet music sounded and joyful cries rang out all around them. Before the girl had time to get over the horror of the other rooms, there was a tremendous clap of thunder, so loud as though the earth and sky were being rent. This was followed by silence and a great stillness. The dark wood, the cave, the horrible animals, the bear—all had vanished, and the merchant's youngest daughter

Look not around, neither to left nor right,
Eyes on the ground and you will be all right.

found herself in a magnificent castle with golden walls and servants in magnificent liveries. The bear had turned into a handsome, young man, prince of that splendid castle, and he now came towards her to claim her as his bride and to thank her for having, by her courage, rescued him and all his servants from the spell that had been put upon them.

The last was worst, full of dragons, snakes, bloated toads, basilisks and winged serpents.

Though now a rich and noble princess, the merchant's daughter always wore the hazel twig in her hair. And the strange thing about it was that the twig never withered, and she wore it all the more gladly because it had proved the key to her happiness.

The prince's young bride hastened to send news to her parents and sisters and tell them what had happened, and shortly afterwards she and the prince sent for them and they all went and lived at the "Bear's Castle" for the rest of their lives.

## VI

# The Enchanted Princess

ONCE there was a poor craftsman who had two sons. One was nice and the other horrid, but as sometimes happens in this peculiar world, the Father loved the nasty one, whose name was Helmrich, more than the nice one, who was called Hans.

The years passed and a time came when the craftsman found that he had been paying out more money than people had been paying him, and that his purse was quite empty. "I must do something about this," the poor man thought. "If my customers will not come to me to pay their bills, I must go to them and ask for my money. It is up to me. I must be polite, but firm." So off he went early each morning knocking at people's doors. But the grandest people are not always the best payers, and no one likes paying bills, so day after day the poor man returned home tired and with his purse as empty as when he had set out. He could not bear to go home and see his wife's long face and worried expression, so he would sit outside the door of the inn, sad and lonely, and not in the mood—even had it been possible—to go inside and join the others.

However, though he sat there by himself, busy with his own gloomy thoughts, he could not help hearing what the others were saying inside. One day, then, he heard a stranger who had just come from the big city, telling some story. At first he listened with only half an ear, then with a whole ear, and finally with both ears, for what the stranger was telling them, was that the king's lovely young daughter had been laid under a spell and made captive by a wicked witch, and she must remain in her prison till someone came who could pass three tests. If anyone did come and manage to pass these difficult tests, the king had promised that he should have the lovely princess's hand, the magnificent castle and all the things in it.

When he heard this the craftsman thought to himself: "My son Helmrich is a smart young chap. He could shave a billy goat's beard, if anyone asked him to, and I'm sure he could pass those tests. Then he would marry the lovely princess and become lord of the land and all its people, and all my troubles would be over."

So, forgetting all about his sorrows and the money people owed him, he hurried home to tell his wife the news. The next morning he told his son Helmrich about it and Helmrich said that he would try his luck, so his father fitted him out with a horse, sword, pistols and fine clothes just as quick as these could be got. As he set out, Helmrich promised that he would soon come in a coach with six horses to fetch them and his stupid brother Hans. He already felt as though he were king.

Helmrich was rather a high-spirited, spiteful youth, and he vented his spite in a very nasty way on all the creatures he met as he went along. He threw sticks and stones at the birds singing their songs in praise of Our Lord and frightened them off their branches. He never came across an animal without scaring it or playing some trick on it. When he saw an ant-heap, he rode his horse at it and made him trample it; then, when the angry ants climbed onto his horse and him, he squashed and killed them all. A little later, he came to a pond on which twelve ducks were swimming. He lured these into the bank and killed them all but one, which managed to escape. Then he came upon a hive of wild bees and destroyed it, as he had done the ant-heap. His greatest pleasure was not to protect innocent creatures, but to torment and destroy them out of sheer spitefulness and nastiness.

In the evening, as the sun was going down, he reached the splendid castle in which the enchanted princess was imprisoned. He knocked loudly on the castle gate. There was no reply. Then he banged more loudly still on the great gate, and in the end a little shutter in the gate opened and an aged, wizened old crone with a face the colour of cobwebs looked out and crossly asked what he wanted.

"I've come to free the princess," Helmrich said. "Open up, go on, hurry up!"

"Not so fast, young fellow, tomorrow will do. I shall expect you here at nine o'clock." Then the shutter was closed again and the old crone was gone.

The next morning at nine o'clock the old woman was standing waiting outside the gate. When she saw Helmrich coming she scattered a jugful of linseed over a stretch of grass and said:

"Pick up all the seeds. I shall come back in an hour and you must have finished by then."

Helmrich thought that a very bad joke, and certainly he was not going to break his back picking up all those seeds, so instead he went for a stroll. As a result, when the old woman came back, she found the jug empty.

"This is bad," she said with a grave face. Then she took twelve little golden bowls from her pocket and threw them into the castle pond. "Get those bowls out. I shall be back in an hour, and you must be finished by then."

Helmrich just laughed and shrugged his shoulders, and went for another stroll. When the old woman came back and found that he had not done that task either, she called out twice: "This is bad, bad." Then she took him by the hand and led him through the gate and across the courtyard and into the great hall of the castle. There sat three figures enveloped in thick white veils.

"Choose, my son, but choose correctly! I shall be back in an hour."

When the old woman returned, Helmrich was still no wiser and had no idea which to choose, so he chose at random:

"I choose the one on the right."

Then all three threw their veils back. The one sitting in the middle was the princess, and right and left of her sat two horrible dragons. One of the dragons seized Helmrich in its curly long talons and threw him through the window into a deep abyss.

\* \* \*

A year had passed since Helmrich had left home to rescue the lovely princess and still his parents waited for him to come driving up in a coach with six spanking horses. In the end they could only believe that some dreadful accident had happened to their son.

"Ah," wailed the unhappy father "if only clumsy Hans had gone instead of our bright lad, it would not have been so bad."

"Father," said Hans, "let me go too. Please, I would like to try, and I must find out what has happened to my brother."

But the father would not hear of it. He told himself that if his clever, bright son had not succeeded, what chance would his clumsy, stupid one have. So, he refused to let Hans have either a horse or weapons.

Hans, however, decided that he would do without, but go he would. So he set off secretly and walked along the road for three days till he came to the castle. He was not in the least bit afraid. At night he slept on soft green moss at the feet of tall old trees and slept as well and as soundly as he did at home. Nor were the birds of the forest frightened of him. On the contrary, they came and sang him their loveliest songs. When he passed the ant-heap that his brother had destroyed, he saw the ants still busy repairing the last of the damage. He even bent down and tried to help them, and those that by mistake crawled up on to him, he carefully picked off and set down on the ground without hurting them. When he came to the pond, he called the ducks to the bank and shared the remains of his bread with them. And when he saw the bees, he plucked some flowers and laid them by the entrance to the hive.

Then, happy at being alive, he reached the castle and knocked shyly on the gate. The shutter opened and the old woman asked him what he wanted.

"If I am not too humble a person," said Hans, "I would very much like to try and rescue the beautiful princess."

At once the great gate was opened and the old woman said:

"Try my son, by all means, but remember that if you cannot pass the three tests, it will cost you your life."

"Never mind, mother, I would like to try," said Hans.

Then the old woman put him to the first test, scattering the linseed and telling him that she would be back in an hour, by which time he must have finished. Hans was not lazy. He bent down and began working feverishly, but, as it seemed, in almost no time at all the three-quarters had struck and the bottom of the jug was little more than covered. Hans was on the point of despairing, when two ants came crawling up, then more and more, and in a moment the ground was black with them. Each picked up a seed and in a moment or two the jug was full. There was not one linseed left anywhere on the grass. When the old woman saw this, she said, "Good. That is good." Then she threw the twelve bowls into the pond. Hans at once plunged into the depths to try and fish the bowls up in time. Yet, however deep he dived, he could never reach the bottom. Desperate, he sat down on the bank and wondered what on earth he could do. Then, looking up, he saw twelve ducklings come swimming up and each held one of the golden bowls in its beak. They came out of the water and laid the bowls on the grass. And so Hans' second task was completed within the time.

When the old woman returned and saw that he had passed the second test, too, she said: "Good, that is very good." Then she took him by the hand and led him through the gate, across the courtyard and into the great hall, where the hardest test of all awaited him. Desperately Hans scrutinized the three veiled figures. He wondered, considered, but could reach no conclusion. Who could help him? His time was nearly up. Then a swarm of bees came flying in through the open window and circled with much buzzing round the veiled figures. It was all too obvious how quickly they flew away from the two figures on the right and left, which they did because the dragons smelled of pitch and sulphur. But round the middle figure they circled slowly and quietly, buzzing in a deep, low tone: "The middle one, middle one, middle one." For the princess was very fond of honey and no doubt smelled sweetly of it.

At the end of the hour, the old woman returned and Hans, quite sure and decided in his own mind, pointed to the middle figure and said: "That is the King's daughter." At that the evil dragons shot through the window at lightning speed and were never seen again. The lovely princess then threw off her veil, rejoicing at being free and pleased to be Hans' bride.

Hans hastened to have the fastest coach in the castle harnessed with a team of six horses, and sent it to fetch his parents, and they all lived happily and free from care to the end of their days.

VII

# The Table, the Donkey and the Cudgel

ONCE in a town, little larger than a village, there lived an honest tailor with his wife and three sons. Although the boys all had proper names like other children, their father and mother never called them by their Christian names, but only Tiny (the tall one), Fatty and Stupid. The years passed and as they grew up, Tiny was apprenticed to a joiner, Fatty to a miller and Stupid to a turner.

When Tiny returned home after serving his apprenticeship, his father sent him off into the wide world so that he might get to know foreign lands and peoples. Gaily he said goodbye and set off out of the town through the arched gateway. He walked on and on and on, but nowhere could he find any work to do. No one seemed to want a joiner. The little money that he had for the journey was fast running out, and it was a glum Tiny that walked along with his head hanging. The road led him to a beautiful, quiet wood, and deep in this wood Tiny met a small, but rather fat little man who gave him a friendly salute and said:

## THE TABLE, THE DONKEY AND THE CUDGEL

"Well, my lad, where are you going? And why are you so glum? What's wrong?"

"I have no work," Tiny answered truthfully. "That's all that's wrong with me. I have travelled far in search of it, and I have almost come to the end of my money."

"What is your trade?" the little man asked.

"I am a joiner," Tiny replied.

"Well, you come with me and I'll give you a job," said the little man. "You see, I live here in the wood. Come along with me and I'll show you everything."

Scarcely a hundred yards away lay a lovely, green house surrounded by a hedge of firs, and by the entrance were two tall fir-trees standing like giant sentries. The little man took Tiny to the house. Tiny soon threw off his sadness. In fact he was in quite a happy mood as he stepped into the snug room into which the little man ushered him.

"Welcome," said a voice from the fireplace, and a little old woman came tripping across the floor and helped Tiny off with his rucksack. Tiny's new master chatted with him all evening, and the little old woman brought them food and set a jug containing what was much better than water or lemonade on the table.

Tiny was very pleased with his job. He did not have overmuch to do, but he worked industriously and behaved so well that nobody could possibly have found fault with him.

After several months, however, the little man said:

"My dear Tiny, unfortunately I have no more work for you and I shall have to give you notice. I have no money to pay you for the work that you have done for me, but instead I will give you a keepsake worth far more than gold or silver." Saying that, he produced a sweet little miniature table and said: "Whenever you stand this table up and say to it three times: 'Table, table, lay thyself,' it will set before you whatever food and drink you feel you would like. So, goodbye and think of us sometimes."

Tiny was reluctant to have to go, and said goodbye sadly. He rejoiced, however, that he had this wonderful little table and thanked his master for it very much. Then he turned his steps homewards.

As he journeyed, the little table fed him. Every time he spoke the magic words, it produced all that he might want, the finest dishes, the choicest wines, whatever he could think of, and all the dishes were of solid silver and always the table was covered with a snow-white cloth. Of course, Tiny was very, very careful of his little table. In the inn where he was to spend the last night before he reached home, however, the innkeeper, wondering why he had ordered no food downstairs, peeped through a crack in the door of the room and discovered the secret of the magic table. Before he went to bed, Tiny brought the little table and asked the innkeeper if he could put it in a safe place for the night as it was very precious, and, of course, the innkeeper said that he would. He took the table and at once made it provide him with a wonderful feast, after which he sat wondering how on earth he could obtain possession of the table and have it for his own. Then he remembered that he had a little table very like the magic one, only it was not magic at all. So, the next morning the cunning innkeeper brought his little table to Tiny's room and gave it to him, having carefully hidden the other.

All unsuspecting, Tiny set off with the wrong little

## THE TABLE, THE DONKEY AND THE CUDGEL

table and strode along gaily, for he knew that he would soon be home.

Joyfully Tiny embraced his father and mother and his two brothers, and gleefully he told them of the wonderful little table he had brought back home. The father thought this very peculiar, in fact he did not believe him. So Tiny fetched his table and said to it thrice: "Table, table, lay thyself!" but it did nothing of the kind. Then the honest old tailor said:

"Are you trying to make a fool of your father? And have you come back with nothing from your long journeyings?"

Poor Tim did not know what to say. He could think of no reason why the magic words had lost their power, why the spell was broken. Whatever the reason, Tiny had to start working for his food again.

Meanwhile Fatty had returned from his time of apprenticeship to the miller, and he too must out into the wide world to see and to learn. By chance he took the same road as his brother and the same thing happened to him. He came to the wood, met the fat little man and was given work. Only now the house in the wood was a mill. After Fatty had been working there for some time, happy and giving every satisfaction, he too was told that his master had no more work and must send him away. As a parting gift the fat little miller gave him a fine donkey and said:

"Take this as a parting present. I cannot give you money for your work, but this donkey will be more use to you than gold or silver. Whenever you say to it: 'Donkey, stretch!' it will sneeze out a shower of gold coins."

Often as Tiny had said to his table: "Table, table,

lay thyself," Fatty cried to his donkey: "Donkey, stretch" even more often. And each time the donkey stretched out his neck and sneezed out a shower of golden ducats that rattled down with a sound that rang most pleasantly in the ears of the tailor's second son. On his way home Fatty too came to the inn with the cunning greedy innkeeper who had robbed his brother of his magic table.

Fatty ordered a sumptuous meal, played host to all the others there in the most generous way in the world, and when the innkeeper presented his bill, which was not a small one, he just said:

"Wait a moment and I will get the money." Then he whipped off the table cloth and went out to the stable. There he spread the tablecoth on the straw where the donkey was standing, cried: "Donkey, stretch!" Then the donkey stretched out his neck, sneezed and golden coins fell clinking into the white cloth. The innkeeper, however, was just outside looking through a knot-hole in the stable wall and he saw and heard all that happened.

The next morning Fatty got up rather late, had his breakfast and went to the stable for his donkey. There it was in its stall, only it was not the right donkey. Fatty, however, did not know that. Gaily he mounted it and rode off knowing that he would soon be home. When he reached home, he told his father of his wonderful good fortune and the magic powers of his donkey. They all gathered round the donkey in the stable, and Fatty pronounced the magic words: "Donkey, stretch!" But the donkey did nothing of the sort. It did not even sneeze, let alone produce any gold coins. Everyone laughed and Fatty felt horribly ashamed and then

## THE TABLE, THE DONKEY AND THE CUDGEL

became very angry. He took a stick and beat the donkey, but it was no good, he could beat no ducats out of it. So Fatty too had to look for work and earn his living as a miller, which he thought he would never need to do again.

Several years passed and the youngest of the tailor's sons, Stupid, returned from his apprenticeship having learned his craft of turner. He was a handsome young fellow, and he now went off to see the world in his turn. On purpose he chose the same road as his brothers had gone, for he too wanted to meet the little man of whom his brothers had spoken as having been so kind and clever and having such wonderful things to give. Sure enough, he reached the same wood and came to the solitary little house there and met the little old man and was given a job.

He too worked conscientiously, but not too hard, and after several months the little man came to him and said, as he had to the others:

"My dear boy, I have no more work for you and cannot keep you on. I must give you notice. I would like to give you something nice, as I did to your brothers. But what can I do for you, when you are called Stupid? Your two brothers, the tall one and the fat one, lost their presents through their own stupidity. So what on earth would happen to you? But take this bag; it may be useful to you. You have only to say to it: 'Cudgel, out of the bag!' and you will have a cudgel to protect you and defend you or help you. It will go on striking and hitting till you say 'Cudgel, into the bag'."

The young turner thanked him politely, shouldered his rucksack and set off homewards. For a long time he had no need to use his cudgel, for when anyone whistles as merrily as he did, he is left in peace. Only now and again did some village dogs come rushing out and bark and snarl at him, and then he summoned his cudgel out of its bag and got it to drive them off. So, in due course, he came to the inn kept by the innkeeper who had robbed his brothers of their presents and who was now leading a carefree life of luxury, but nonetheless had no objection to purloining further things from other travellers.

Before he went to bed, the turner gave the innkeeper the bag with the cudgel, telling him that it was very valuable and warning him most emphatically not to say "Cudgel, out of the bag", since, he ought to know, it had a very peculiar characteristic that would give a lot to whoever said it.

The innkeeper had profited so much from the magic table and donkey of which he robbed the other two brothers, that he was very keen to possess a third such wonder-working object. He could scarcely wait till the turner had got upstairs, and then he cried: "Cudgel, out of the bag." At once the cudgel rushed out and began beating a tattoo on the innkeeper's back, it hit him there and everywhere, till he was black and blue all over and he began yelling most pitifully and ran howling to the turner.

"Innkeeper, it serves you right," said the turner. "I warned you! You robbed my brothers of their magic table and donkey."

The innkeeper wailed and screeched: "Come, help me, I shall be killed. I will give it all back, the magic table and the donkey—I shall drop—I shall die."

So then the turner called out: "Cudgel, into the

## THE TABLE, THE DONKEY AND THE CUDGEL

At once the cudgel rushed out and began beating a tattoo on the innkeeper's back.

bag!" and the cudgel at once crept back obediently. The innkeeper was delighted to have escaped with his life and he gave Stupid the table and donkey. So Stupid packed his things together, tied his bundle on the donkey and set off for home.

Imagine the delight of the two older brothers when they saw their precious presents and that they would still work their magic. The one they had to thank for this was the young brother whom they had always called Stupid, yet he had proved sharper and more clever than they.

The three brothers lived on with their parents and none of them ever needed to work for his living again. From then on they had everything that their hearts desired.

## VIII

# The Tale of the Hard Heart

WHETHER or not you believe in gnomes, goblins, ogres, fairies and others of the little people, the inhabitants of the Black Forest most certainly do and one of them even had a remarkable experience with them. He was the son of a widow, Mrs. Barbara Munkin, whose husband had been a charcoal-burner. His name was Peter.

Peter became a charcoal-burner like his father, but charcoal burning is a craft that leaves you lots of time for thinking, and Peter found, as he sat alone by his pile surrounded by the dark trees and the silence of the forest, that he became filled with vague longings that left him feeling discontented. Finally he came to the conclusion that what was wrong with him was his trade. He did not like being a charcoal-burner, which made you dirty and kept you living all by yourself in the gloomy forest for weeks on end. And when he did go to the local inn in his best clothes, people just said: "Oh, it's only Peter, the charcoal-burner!" At the inn he used to see lumbermen who took the timber rafts to the sea, playing for high stakes, losing and winning more in an evening at cards than Peter earned in a whole year, and Peter was jealous, very jealous.

One day Peter suddenly remembered how as a child he had heard his father and others speak of Dutch Michael and the Little Glass Man and how those two could make you rich. There was a verse, he remembered, that you had to recite at a certain spot in the middle of the forest, and the Little Glass Man would appear, provided you had been born on a Sunday between eleven and two—and Peter had. However, he could only remember the first three lines. and there were four. Nevertheless, one day Peter put on his best clothes and walked and walked till he came to the highest part of the forest where the trees grew very tall, hoping that three lines would work the spell. Standing at the foot of a huge and immensely tall tree, he took off his hat and said: "Good evening, sir!" Then he spoke the three lines he knew.

Almost at once Peter thought he saw a tiny figure emerge and dart behind another tree. He called out, waited, but nothing further happened. All that he could see was a squirrel playing in the big tree. Again and again Peter tried, but at last he turned and walked sadly away. Coming to a forester's hut, he asked if they could provide him with a meal, and soon he was sitting at table with the man and his family. After supper as the forester's wife was clearing away, she sang. Her song suddenly reminded Peter of the ending of the fourth line of his verse. That surely must be enough, he thought and quickly paying for his meal, he put on his hat, took up his stick and hurried back into the forest.

It was morning before Peter got back to where he

had been before, and there he recited his verse. "That's not quite right," said a little voice, "but seeing it's you, it will do." Looking round, Peter saw a tiny old man with red stockings and a black coat sitting on a log. He had a nice, friendly face and a beard as fine as gossamer. He was smoking a pipe of blue glass, and when Peter went near, he saw to his amazement that the man's clothes, shoes and hat were all made of coloured glass.

"Sir," said Peter with a bow, "I have come to ask your advice. Things are bad with me. A charcoal-burner cannot get on. I am young and feel that I ought to be able to do something better, especially when I see others at the inn and the amount of money they have."

"Peter," said the little man, "you must not despise your craft. Your father and your grandfather were charcoal-burners and they were happy men. Money is not everything."

"Perhaps not," said Peter, "but I would like to be something better than a charcoal-burner, so that people didn't say 'Oh, it's only Peter'."

"I don't like it," said the little man, "but, like the others who have come to me, you shall have three wishes. The first two shall be what you like; the third I may refuse if it is silly."

"Oh, how wonderful!" said Peter. "Well, let me see: first I should like to dance better than the one we at the inn call the king of the dance floor, and always to have as much money in my pocket as old fat Ezekiel."

"You idiot," said the little man. "What a pitiable wish! I hope that the next one will be more sensible."

Peter scratched his head and, after a little hesitation, said: "Well, I wish I owned the best and richest glassworks in all the Black Forest with all that goes with it and the money to run it."

"Nothing else, Peter? Nothing else?" said the little man.

"Well, you could—you could add a horse and a little carriage."

"Oh, you silly fool," exclaimed the Little Glass Man, who was so angry that he dashed his pipe against a fir tree so that it splintered into a thousand pieces. "Sense and intelligence are what you should have asked for. But never mind, it wasn't such a bad wish."

"But I still have a wish left," said Peter. "I could ask for that now."

"No you don't," replied the little man. "You will get into fixes enough, when you'll be glad you have a wish in hand. Now, off home with you! Here is two thousand guilders and don't come to me for money again. Three days ago old Winkfritz who had the big glassworks at Unterwald died and the works are for sale. Go there early tomorrow and make a bid. Be good and work hard, and I'll come and see you sometimes. But, beware of the inn and don't spend much time there. Your first wish was a bad and stupid one."

As he spoke, the little man had taken out another pipe of the finest alabaster glass, filled it with dried fir needles and put it into his toothless mouth. Then he pulled out an enormous magnifying glass, stepped into the sunlight and lit his pipe. Then he shook Peter's hand, said goodbye and, puffing at his pipe, faster and faster, suddenly vanished in a cloud of smoke.

The next day Peter went to the glassworks in Unterwald. A price was soon agreed, and Peter became the owner. He kept on all the workmen, and at first he took a real interest in all that was done; but gradually he took to coming to the works every other day, then only once a week, and as a result his men did just as they pleased, while Peter spent his time at the inn. There Peter was treated with all the deference due to a man who could leap higher and step more nimbly than the king of the dance floor himself, and who could stake as highly and lose as much as old Ezekiel could win.

Meanwhile the factory was making glass day and night, but Peter did not know how to sell it; instead he sold it at half price to wandering pedlars and such folk, just in order to get money to pay his workmen's wages. Because he attended to nothing, business went from bad to worse, and soon his debts were so large that Peter was very worried and anxious indeed. One evening as he was walking back from the inn, thinking about these dreary things, he felt that he was not alone. Looking down he saw the Little Glass Man walking beside him.

"It's all your fault!" Peter exclaimed when he saw him. "Before, I was happy and had no worries. Now I don't know what to do. I can't sell my glass, and my creditors are threatening to sell me up."

"Indeed," said the little man, "it's my fault, is it? Is that all the thanks I get for my kindness to you? Who asked you to make such stupid wishes? You wanted to have a glassworks and you have. But sense is what you needed most, Peter—sense."

"What do you mean?" exclaimed Peter angrily. "I'm as clever as the next man. I'll show you," and, saying that, Peter seized the Little Glass Man by the collar and shouted: "Now, I've got you. Now I'll have my third wish—250,000 thalers, here on the spot and a horse and—oh, oh, oh!" Peter yelled and shook his hand violently, for the little man had turned himself into molten glass and burned Peter's hand badly. And now he was nowhere to be seen.

Peter's swollen hand reminded him of the little man for a long time. Peter drowned his sorrows at the inn and felt that things could never be too bad, as long as Ezekiel had money, for then Peter had too. One day, however, Ezekiel's luck was out and he began to lose. He lost and lost all evening, and when he had nothing left at all and his pockets were quite empty, he asked Peter to lend him some money. "With pleasure," said Peter, "as much as you like." But when he put his hand into his own pocket, he found that it was empty too—he had just as much in his pocket as old Ezekiel had, which was what he had wished.

The next morning when Peter went to the works, he found the bailiff there with a long list of all Peter's debts. "Can you pay?" asked the bailiff. Peter had to admit that he could pay nothing at all, so the glass-works, his house, his horse and the carriage, everything was taken from him. Peter had nothing.

If this is all the Little Glass Man can do for me, thought Peter, I'll try Dutch Michael next; so that very day he went into the depths of the forest to the place of which he knew, and when he got there, called out: "Dutch Michael! Mr. Dutch Michael!" The next moment he saw in front of him the enormous figure of Dutch Michael. "Oh, there you are, Peter!" said Dutch Michael, "I have been expecting you Come in. I am sure we shall be able to make a deal."

Wondering what he could have that Dutch Michael wanted, Peter followed the giant down in a deep, vast chasm and so into a great room where everything was enormous—the clock on the wall, the stove, the seats and table, everything was huge, because Dutch Michael was at least a head taller than the tallest man Peter had ever seen.

"What's wrong with you, Peter," said Dutch Michael, "is that you feel things."

"It is indeed," said Peter.

"Where do you feel them most?" asked Dutch Michael.

"Here," said Peter, laying his hand on his heart.

"Just as I thought," said Dutch Michael. "People are much better off without hearts. Look over there." Peter turned and saw shelf upon shelf filled with jars, in each of which, in some clear liquid, was a heart. Each jar was labelled and Peter read the names of old Ezekiel, the king of the dance floor, the bailiff and of most of the notables for miles around. "Give me your heart," said Dutch Michael, "and you can have what you want. Shall we say a hundred thousand guilders to start with?" "But I must have a heart," said Peter, "I'd die without one." "You shall have this instead," said Dutch Michael, producing a beautifully shaped heart of stone. "It's pleasantly cool, never pounds or gets agitated, and leaves you quite unmoved. I can recommend it."

"Does it work?" asked Peter.

"Perfectly," said Dutch Michael.

"Done!" said Peter.

Dutch Michael then produced glasses and a bottle of wine and they began to drink. Soon Peter felt drowsy and finally he fell asleep. When he woke up, he found himself in an elegant carriage, driving along a fine highway away from the Black Forest and all he had known as home. He was dressed in smart new clothes and hardly knew himself. Yet somehow he felt neither joy nor sorrow, not even when he thought of his mother and that she must be worried about him. In the coach were various suits of clothes, in fact all that he could possibly need, and a bag containing several thousand thalers.

So Peter drove into the wide world and travelled thus for two years. But the only things that he really enjoyed were drink and sleep. The beauty of the countryside, or of buildings, left him unmoved; he could find no pleasure in music or dancing. Nothing moved his heart of stone. He even seemed to have forgotten how to laugh.

After two years Peter returned home. The first person he went to see was Dutch Michael, to whom he complained that life had lost its savour. Everything bored him and he seemed to find pleasure in nothing. "What you need to do," said Dutch Michael, "is to build yourself a house, find a wife and start some business to keep you occupied." And Dutch Michael gave him another hundred thousand thalers to start his business with. Peter thought this sound advice and went off again to the inn, where he thought he would stay till his house was ready. Of course, the news soon spread that Peter was back, richer than ever.

Peter built himself a house and filled it with lovely things. He was no longer interested in glass, but dealt in wood and corn, lending money out at high rates and selling dear to people who could not pay cash and had to have credit. Now he never gave to beggars or the poor, and he even refused to help his own mother who was poor and old. When she came to his door, he might send a servant with a few small coins, but he could never be bothered even to go and speak to her, and he never asked her in.

So Peter became richer and richer, and finally he decided that he would get himself a wife. There was no father who would not gladly have given his daughter to rich Peter, but Peter had great difficulty in finding a girl who was lovely enough to be his wife. At last he heard of a forester's daughter who was said to be the most beautiful of all the girls in the Black Forest, and as good as she was lovely, and when he went to her father's cottage, he found that it was so indeed. And Peter married her and took her to live in his magnificent house.

Lisbeth, Peter's wife, was loving and kind; she had a very tender heart and she could never bring herself to obey her husband's order that nothing must ever be given away, even to beggars or the poor. One day Peter found her giving bread and wine to a poor old man who had collapsed under a great load of wood he had been carrying. The wine happened to be some of Peter's very best, and he was so furious that he struck Lisbeth on the forehead with the knob of his cane and she dropped to the ground. The old man, however, was really the Little Glass Man and he was so angry with Peter that he picked him up and flung him to the ground, knocking him unconscious.

When Peter eventually came to, he could not see Lisbeth anywhere. He searched for her everywhere, but she had disappeared. Peter's stony heart did not feel sorry for what he had done, yet he did not feel right. Then one night in a dream he heard his wife's sweet voice saying: "Peter, get yourself a warmer heart!" Night after night, the same thing happened, and in the end Peter thought there was something in it, so he went to the place in the forest and spoke the magic verse. Again the Little Glass Man appeared, not at all friendly now, and Peter reminded him that he still had a wish left. The Little Glass Man agreed, and reminded Peter that he could refuse it if it were stupid. Then Peter asked that he might be given his heart back again. This the little Glass Man could not do, only Dutch Michael could do that, but he told Peter of a way in which he might trick Dutch Michael, who was really rather stupid, into giving him his heart again, and he also gave Peter a glass cross that would protect him against Dutch Michael's strength.

So Peter went to Dutch Michael and, pretending that he wanted more money in order to leave the country, because he had killed his wife, was taken to Dutch Michael's house. There he accused the giant of not being able to work magic properly, because he could sometimes feel his heart, and said that the heart in the jar that was supposed to be his was just made of wax. In the end Dutch Michael became so angry that he said that he would prove to Peter that the heart in the jar was Peter's. He tore off Peter's jacket, opened up Peter's chest and very carefully replaced his proper heart from the jar. The moment his true heart was in place, Peter produced the glass cross and Dutch Michael, though furious, was powerless to prevent him leaving with his own proper heart still in place.

Peter then went back to the Little Glass Man. Now

that he had his proper heart, Peter was overcome with grief and the thought of all the misery he had caused, and, most of all, how he had behaved to his mother and perhaps even killed his wife, Lisbeth, for whom he now felt a great love. The Little Glass Man asked Peter what he wanted, and Peter said that he wanted nothing. Neither his mother nor his wife could possibly forgive him and nothing else mattered. Peter wanted nothing except to die. The Little Glass Man gave him a long look, then he knocked out his pipe, stuffed it in his pocket and walked behind a tree.

For a long time Peter sat with his head in his hands; then he heard the Little Glass Man say: "Look round, Peter." Peter did so and saw his mother and Lisbeth standing there, looking at him with love in their eyes. Peter jumped to his feet. "So you are not dead, Lisbeth!" he exclaimed joyfully. "And do you and you, Mother, forgive me?" "They will forgive you, Peter," said the Little Glass Man, "because you are truly sorry. Go now to your father's cottage and be a charcoal-burner again as once you were. If you work well and live decently, people will like and respect you far more than they did when you were rich."

Then the three turned and walked to the cottage that had been Peter's father's and which was not far away. As it happened the rich house Peter had built himself was that day struck by lightning and burned to the ground with everything in it.

When they reached the cottage in the forest, they found that it had become a little farmhouse and everything needful was in it, simple, but new and bright. There they lived and Lisbeth liked it far better than the big house with many servants; in fact, they were all happier than they had ever been. Peter worked hard and cleverly, and before long they had all that they needed. When Peter was old and grey, he often used to tell his children how much better it is to love and be loved and have little, than to be rich and have a hard heart.

# IX

# The Three Dogs

ONCE there was a shepherd, a very poor shepherd who was also a widower, and he had two children, a son and a daughter, and the three lived together in a tiny little house at the foot of a hill outside a tiny little village in a wild and rather desolate part of the country. Then the poor shepherd fell ill and had to go to bed. He got worse and worse and in the end he died, leaving his two children all that he possessed, the tiny little house and three sheep. As he lay dying the shepherd called his two children to him and said to them: "Divide everything between you and let there be no dispute or quarrelling." Then, when the poor shepherd had died, the boy said to his sister: "Which would you rather have: the house or the sheep?" The girl replied that she would rather have the house, whereupon her brother said:

"All right, you take the house and I will take the sheep and go off into the wide world where so many have found their fortune and happiness. Perhaps I shall be lucky, for after all I was born on a Sunday."

So the brother took the three sheep, his only inheritance, and set off into the wide world, leaving his sister in the tiny house that had also been his home. Fortune, however, seemed very difficult to find and nowhere did he encounter any traces of her. One day he was sitting rather gloomily at a cross-roads wondering what he should do and which way he should go, when he looked up and found that he was no longer alone. He now had the company of a man, a strange man who was now sitting beside him, and at whose feet lay three black dogs, one bigger than the others.

"Hallo, young fellow," said the man. "You have three very fine sheep there; did you know that? In fact," the man went on, "if you will give me your sheep, I will give you my dogs in exchange."

Although he felt so sad, the boy had to laugh when he heard this suggestion.

"What should I do with your three dogs?" he asked. "My sheep feed themselves, but your dogs would expect me to feed them."

"My dogs are not quite ordinary dogs," said the strange man, bending down and patting their shaggy black heads, "they will feed you instead of you having to feed them; in fact, they will make your fortune. The little one here is called 'Food-bringer', the second 'Tearer' and this big, strong one 'Iron-and-steel breaker'. Food-bringer will bring you food whenever you tell him to do so, Tearer will tear anyone to pieces at your command, and Iron-and-steel breaker will do just that if ever you should require it."

The boy was still not convinced, but in the end he agreed to make the exchange. Somewhat reluctantly he gave the sheep to the stranger, who at once drove them off and vanished from sight. The boy then thought that he would test the dogs and see if they really could do what the stranger had said. So he called Food-bringer and said to him: "Bring food!"; and the dog at once ran off. In no time at all, it seemed, Foodbringer was back, wagging his tail and carrying a large basket which proved to be filled with the loveliest food, beautiful chicken and all sorts of delicacies that the shepherd's son had never even tasted before. After that he was glad that he had made the exchange.

So the shepherd boy happily roamed the country with his three dogs, enjoying the lovely summer weather and eating such heavenly meals as he had never dared dream of. One day he happened to see coming towards him a coach drawn by two black horses and driven by a coachman in black hat and coat. Inside sat a beautiful girl also dressed in black. The girl was weeping most bitterly, and the horses were walking along slowly with hanging heads, as though they too were sad.

When the coach drew level, the shepherd called to the coachman and asked who he was driving, where he was going and why were they so sad. The coachman answered crossly, and would say nothing, but the boy kept on asking and in the end the coachman told him that in that part of the country lived a great dragon which, every year, demanded tribute of a maiden in order to stop it laying the country waste. Every year lots were drawn to decide which of the country's maidens of fourteen were to be given to the dragon, and this year the lot had fallen upon the King's own daughter. Because of this, the King and the whole country were plunged in grief, but the dragon had to have its victim.

The shepherd boy felt dreadfully sorry for the lovely young girl and followed the coach on its way. At length the coachman reined in the horses at the foot of a tall mountain. The girl got out and began walking slowly up the mountain to meet the fate that awaited her. The coachman saw the strange youth set off after her and warned him not to go, but the youth just walked on.

When the girl had climbed almost half way up the mountainside, a fearsome monster came down from

The king's daughter had fainted.

the summit. It had a scaly body, leathery wings and horrid great talons on its feet, while a blast of hot, sulphurous vapour came from its fiery throat. It was just about to fling itself upon the trembling girl, when the young stranger called to Tearer, the second of his dogs, and said to him: "Tear it!" and at once the shaggy black dog hurled itself at the monster and plunged its teeth into the soft part of the dragon's throat. Hard as the dragon struggled to shake Tearer off, the dog hung on and worried the dragon so that

At once the shaggy black dog hurled itself at the monster.

in the end the great monster collapsed and lay there, dead. At once the dog began to eat the dead dragon, and so gorged itself on it that all that was left was a few of the dragon's teeth, and these the shepherd lad put in his pocket.

Meanwhile, the King's daughter had fainted and

now the shepherd lad bathed her temples with cool water and revived her. Then the King's daughter thanked him as well as she could and begged him most earnestly to go with her back to her father, who would wish to reward her rescuer. However, the shepherd lad said first that he must see the world, as he had set out to do; but in three years he would return and then he would gladly come to see her and her father. The Princess tried her hardest to make him change his mind, but he would not, and, whistling to his three dogs, he set off on his way again, while the maiden went back to her coach and drove home feeling happier than she could ever remember being.

The coachman, however, was not a good man, and he now thought of a wicked plan. As they were driving across a bridge beneath which ran a broad, fierce torrent, he stopped the coach and turning to the King's daughter said:

"Your rescuer has gone and has no need of your gratitude nor of any reward. It would be nice, however, if you were to make some poor fellow happy in thanks for your rescue, so when you get back, tell your father that it was I who killed the dragon and let me have the reward. If you will not promise to do that, then I shall throw you into the torrent here and now. Everybody thinks the dragon has eaten you, so no one will miss you or ask questions."

What was the maiden to do? She pleaded and pleaded, but it was all to no purpose, and finally she had to promise to pretend that the coachman had rescued her and that she would tell no one the truth. Having received her promise, the coachman whipped up the horses and they drove back to the city.

## THE THREE DOGS

There everyone was overjoyed to see the princess safe and sound; the black flag flying from the tower was quickly pulled down, the bells were rung and the streets filled with cheering people. The King hugged and kissed his daughter and could not find words enough to thank the man who said he had rescued her.

"You have not only saved my daughter, but rescued the whole country from a cruel plague," the King said. "Therefore it is only right that I reward you accordingly. My daughter shall become your wife; but as she is still so young, the wedding shall not be for another year."

The coachman thanked the King, as well he might. He was provided with magificent clothes, given a noble title and taught all the things a man of position and the future husband of the King's daughter ought to know and be able to do. The King's daughter, however, was horrified and wept most bitterly when she was told what her father had decided; yet she did not dare break her promise and tell the truth.

So time passed and soon the year was almost up. The young Princess went to her father and pleaded for another year, and as she was still so young and her father loved her, he granted her request. When this second year was all but over, the Princess, remembering that her true rescuer had said that he would return in three years, threw herself at her father's feet and begged him to put the wedding off for one more year. The King was unable to refuse her pleading and granted her another year, but said that it must be the last and that after that she really must marry as he had arranged.

All too quickly this third year passed. The date of the wedding was fixed and soon it was near at hand. The streets were all beflagged and the city full of visitors come to see and take part in the festivities. On the very morning of the betrothal banquet, a young man came to the city, a young man who had three black and shaggy dogs. Seeing the streets beflagged and crowded, the young man asked the reason and was told that it was because the King's daughter was about to marry the man who had rescued her from the dragon. When he heard this, the new arrival said loudly that the man she was to marry was a fraud, a cheat who was pretending to have done what another had accomplished. The people were so horrified at what they heard that they sent for the watch, and the young man was arrested and taken to prison, where he was put into a cell with an iron door and iron bars at the window. There he sat on a bundle of straw thinking what an unlucky fellow he was, when all at once he thought he could hear a sound of whining, a whimpering as though his dogs were there. Then he had an idea.

"Iron-and-steel-breaker" he called as loud as he could. The next moment he heard a scrabbling sound, then two large black paws appeared at the window through which a faint light filtered into the cell. Before long the dog had gnawed through the iron bars and jumped down into the cell, where it at once set about chewing through the iron fetters which held its master. Having accomplished that, it jumped out through the window and its master was able to follow.

The young man was now free, but it grieved him to think how another was to be rewarded for what he had done. Then he realized that it was long since he had eaten and that he was ravenous; so, calling Foodbringer, he told it to fetch him food and saw it run off. Soon the dog was back carrying in its mouth a napkin in which were wrapped a selection of delectable things, while the napkin itself had a crown embroidered in one corner.

The King and his Court had been sitting at table, when the dog had suddenly entered the banqueting hall and, going to the Princess, had licked her hand and gazed at her with a beseeching look in its eyes. To her mingled horror and delight the Princess had recognized the dog and realized that her rescuer had come, as he had said he would. As a sign to him, she tied her own napkin round the dog's neck, whereupon it had vanished. Thinking that the appearance of the dog must be a sign from Heaven, the Princess told her father that she must speak to him in private, and as soon as they were alone, she told him the whole story. The King at once sent a page to look for the dog and bring the stranger to the palace. It was not very long before the page returned and ushered a handsome young man into the room where the King was waiting. When the King had heard the young man's story, he took him by the hand and led him into the banqueting hall. At the sight of him the former coachman went as white as a sheet. Realizing that he had been found out, he confessed and, kneeling down, begged for mercy. The Princess confirmed that the young man was the one who really had rescued her, and if further proof were needed, her rescuer was able to show the dragon's teeth which he always carried on him.

The coachman was stripped of his finery and thrown

into a dungeon, and the young man took his place at the Princess's side. This time the King's daughter did not want any postponement of her wedding, which took place the very next day.

The young couple were blissfully happy, and the King's daughter paid special attention to the dogs to whom she owed so much. One day, the young man remembered his sister and said that he would like her to share in his happiness and good fortune. The Princess agreed, so they sent a coach and two footmen to fetch her. Before long the coach returned and brother and sister fell into each other's arms. At that, one of the dogs began to speak.

"Our work is done," it said. "You have no more need of us now. We only stayed with you till we saw whether you would remember your sister in your happiness and good fortune."

Thereupon all three dogs suddenly vanished.

# X

# The Snake King

THE Snake King lived in a big island in the Baltic Sea. His castle was on a tiny island in the middle of a lake which lay near the centre of this big island. It was built underground beneath a hillock and inside it was lovely, shimmering and gleaming with gold and silver jewels. There lived the Snake King, who was a prince transformed into a snake, waiting for his release from the spell that had been put upon him.

Now the Snake King had been transformed into a snake because he had been vain and heartless. He had been an exceptionally handsome young Prince and many Princesses and noble girls had fallen in love with him; but he had never loved any of them. His punishment was to make him learn what it was not to be loved, and so he had to live and crawl as a snake for ever, unless he could find some innocent young girl to take pity on him and kiss him without shrinking or feeling afraid. He had been allowed to keep the colours of the clothes he had been wearing when he was turned into a snake, a silk coat with green and yellow stripes, and so he now had a skin with beautiful green and yellow stripes and wore a gold crown on his head. Otherwise he was a snake, and he could not speak, but hissed. But on certain days of the year, he was allowed to sing, and then his voice was so sweet and lovely that many a poor girl had been entranced and induced to follow him to his castle; yet he had never found one who could really like him and kiss him without shuddering. These poor girls had to stay in the Snake King's castle, where they were to become the servants of the one who released him, if he ever found her.

Not far from the lake in which this little island lay, was a village. The shores of the lake were grassy and the village children used to drive their cows there to graze. Among these children were two with whom our story is concerned, Margaret, who was fourteen, and Jacob, who was sixteen. They had been companions all their lives and loved each other very dearly. They, and the other children who herded their cows by the lake, often saw the Snake King, and they liked him because he was colourful and pretty and his crown sparkled so gaily. The cunning snake often swam across the lake and twined and coiled in the grass and wound his handsome, slim body round the trees and bushes near the children, and the children enjoyed watching him, but they never went very close, because they still had a slight horror of him, though they knew that he never bit or did any harm. Nor had they ever heard him sing, though they had been told that he could and that that was how he had enticed many a poor girl to his castle. Of course, the Snake King could not sing every day, and, besides, he was far too clever to sing when there were several children there, for he could scarcely hope to charm them all. No, when it was his time for singing and he could find a girl alone, then he would sing; and usually he managed to entice the poor girl away.

## THE SNAKE KING

One day Margaret and Jacob were sitting by themselves near some bushes with their cows not far away, when word came that Jacob was to go home quickly. He kissed Margaret, asked her to see to his cows until he got back and ran off home.

Scarcely was Jacob out of sight, when the Snake King came swimming across the lake. He came out of the water and twisted and coiled across the grass, making the loveliest patterns. The golden crown gleamed brightly on his head, his eyes were smiling and his whole demeanour was so sweet and engaging that Margaret was entranced. Nearer and nearer the snake came; then he climbed into a green tree in front of Margaret and swung from the branches there. Then, all at once, he began singing in a voice that was sweet and moving beyond belief. It was as if a thousand nightingales had struck up. Margaret was spellbound and listened without moving. The snake sang a special song, the Bride Song of the Snake King, in which he promised Margaret gold rings, a golden room, jewels, lovely food and wines, clothes and servants galore, if she would go with him. It was a long song and when he had finished, he came down from the tree and began circling round and round where Margaret sat in the grass, singing very softly and sweetly, "Come with me! Come with me!" And Margaret went.

She got to her feet and began to walk towards the lake, but she had not gone far before she remembered all the tales she had heard about the Snake King and wanted to turn back. But it was too late. She was already in the Snake King's power: he coiled round her and carried her across the grass to the lake. She called out: "Jacob! Jacob! Help! Help!" and she shouted to the other children herding their cows further away, but there was no one there to hear or to help her, and the Snake King bore her along like lightning and swam with her across the lake.

Margaret fainted and had no knowledge of how she reached the little island in the lake. When she came to, she found herself in a lovely garden with the most glorious flowers and beautiful trees laden with fruit, but perhaps the strangest thing of all was that she was quite dry, neither her hair not her clothes had got wet in the least. Margaret walked on through the garden, and so came to the door leading to the Snake King's palace. As Margaret appeared, a crowd of girl servants emerged carrying candles and lamps, and they led her into a high marble hall, its walls studded with gold and silver and precious stones. They dressed her in garments of gold and silver and set a golden crown on her head; and then they spoke to her, they called her "Queen" and "Mistress", and they ran and brought her whatever she required. These servants were all young and wore snow-white clothes and had green garlands in their hair. Most of them looked sad, rather than happy.

When night fell, other servants came and led Margaret into a room that gleamed and glistened as though everything was made of gold. In the middle stood a golden bed; the pillows and covers were of pink and blue silk. Most deferentially the servants undressed Margaret, took the shoes from her feet, the crown from her head, and settled her in the bed. Then they turned out all the lamps but one, and withdrew.

It was not long before there was a slithering and a whispering and scraping at the door. Then slowly the door opened and in came the Snake King. He crawled up to Margaret's bed, and whispering and hissing he welcomed her to his palace and, wheedling and persuading, begged her to kiss him and be nice to him. "For then," said the Snake King, "I shall be released from my enchantment and you shall be a rich and a great Queen. For it is my awful fate that I must stay a snake and crawl upon the ground, until I find an innocent girl who will like me and put her arms round me and kiss me; then I shall be turned back into a prince, as I used to be." He hissed low and softly, trying to make it most persuasive, and his eyes sparkled as he raised his head. To Margaret, it looked as though he were going to try and climb into her bed and she shrieked and cried out: "Go away! You horrid, disgusting thing. Never, never will I be your Queen, even if you were as handsome as you are ugly now. I want no one but Jacob." And the Snake King had to turn and go.

In the morning the servants who had undressed Margaret returned and dressed her in the magnificent clothes she had worn before and again set the golden crown on her head. All that day she roamed about the castle and the gardens, which were encircled by a high crystal wall so that she could not go out, and nowhere did she see any sign of the Snake King, which delighted her highly. She was really most unhappy, and whenever she thought of Jacob she burst into tears.

When night fell Margaret was again taken to the golden room and placed in the golden bed, and again the Snake King came as soon as the servants had withdrawn and begged her to put her arms round him and kiss him. That just made Margaret angry and she shouted at him and drove him away.

This same thing happened on the third and fourth nights. And a fifth time the Snake King tried, but that was the finish of it. Sadly the Snake King summoned the servants, who took Margaret's magnificent clothes away and led her to another room. Then the Snake King said to her: "From now on you are just a servant, for such is the order of things here; you can never become Queen now, even if you wished; but you must wait till the time comes and then serve the one who is to be Queen. Go now and join all the others who, like you, have scorned me and my love."

So, after that, Margaret wore a white tunic and a green chaplet like the other servants. They had lots of good food and could roam and play in the garden, and there was almost no work to do, but they found that time hung very heavy on their hands, and they all longed for their homes.

\* \* \*

When Jacob had returned to where he had left Margaret and found her gone, he searched for her high and low. None of the others had seen her, and she was nowhere to be found. A man who had been ploughing near the lake said that he had heard someone calling in the distance and that probably had been poor Margaret. Everyone was sure that the Snake King had carried her off. Jacob was very sad indeed.

Two years passed and then a shepherd happened to tell Jacob how you could become master of enchanted princes and princesses, and even of witches and wizards however bad they were. Jacob at once hurried into the woods and, as the shepherd had told him, cut a stout stick from a bush called the Thorn of the Cross, and on this he carved a cross with his knife. The next time he saw the Snake King making his way over the grass, Jacob plucked up courage and went after him. The Snake King wondered what the lad was up to, for he was quite unused to being attacked, as most people fled from him. As Jacob came nearer, the Snake King thought to himself: "I'll soon make him take to his heels," so he rose up, eyes flashing and tongue darting, the crown on his head red with anger, and hissed and swayed, as though he were about to attack Jacob. But Jacob just came on, saying: "Come on then, you heathen king. I'm not afraid of you." And so the Snake King did attack, but Jacob just touched him lightly with his thorn stick and, wonder of wonders, the Snake King coiled up and twined round the thorn stick like ivy round a tree. Jacob was delighted and cried: "Hold on, my fine one. I must try my trick." Then he took the stick and swung it three times round his head, so that it swished through the air. The Snake King hung on, as if he had grown to the stick. The stick is a good one, thought Jacob. What that shepherd said was true. Then to the Snake King he said: "Snake King if you will give me Margaret back, I will let you go, but not otherwise. Will you give her back?" But the Snake King just shook his head. Then said Jacob: "All right. Goodbye for the present. I shall leave you to spend the night here in the cold and perhaps you will have changed your mind in the morning." Jacob then took the thorn stick and planted it firmly in the ground, and there it stood with the Snake King coiled round it looking rather silly. Then Jacob went home.

In the morning Jacob returned and asked the Snake King if he would release Margaret, but the Snake King just shook his head more decisively than ever. That made Jacob angry, and he went to a bush and cut himself a switch and gave the Snake King quite a thrashing. But the Snake King still refused to nod as a sign that he would give Margaret back, and again Jacob left him there for the night.

The next morning, the Snake King had still not changed his mind, and so Jacob gave him another beating; but still the Snake King would not agree to release Margaret. That night it was bitterly cold and also the Snake King was becoming very hungry and thirsty indeed, so that by the time Jacob returned in the morning, grasping an even heavier switch than before, the Snake King nodded his head three times: he agreed. Jacob made him swear to free not only Margaret but all his other girl captives as well, and then he took his knife and sliced off the cross which he had carved on the thorn stick. At once the Snake King fell from the stick and was free. Then, praying a silent prayer, Jacob mounted the Snake King's back and was borne across the grass to the lake into which the snake plunged. In a moment, it seemed, they had reached the little island in the middle.

The Snake King came to the gate in the high wall that none but he could open, touched it with his head and at once the gate swung open, and in they both went. Jacob soon found his Margaret, and how happy they were to be together again. And how happy were all the others when they heard that they were to be freed as well! Jacob told them that they would leave in two hours, and there was a joyful bustle as they all hurried to pack and get ready. Only the Snake King was sad, and Jacob comforted him, telling him that as none of the girls could free him from his spell, it did not matter if they did go; and Jacob gave the Snake King good advice, telling him to stop being cunning and wily, as that would never get him free. He must learn to be nice and likeable, and then perhaps he would find someone to like and free him from his enchantment.

When Margaret and the other girls were ready, Jacob called to the Snake King: "Open up!" and the Snake King darted his head at the great gate and it swung open, and they all walked out, the Snake King with them. So they came to the water and of course there was no bridge across to the land, and no boat. Then Jacob called: "Hurry up, Snake King, make us a bridge!" But the Snake King could not resist trying one more trick, so he threw a single strand of shimmering cobweb across to the other side and, smiling, said: "I cannot help you. This is the only bridge by which you can cross from this island to the land." He was hoping, of course, that no one would dare set foot on it, in case they should be drowned, and that thus all the girls would have to stay where they were and still be his servants, and then he would have Jacob as well. But Jacob was not to be tricked like that. Taking Margaret by the hand, he cried out: "In God's name, follow me!" and set foot on the gossamer bridge and Margaret after him. At that very moment the gossamer thread turned into a wide, stout bridge of marble arching across the water to the other side. Across this they all passed safely, and as the last set foot on the far side, the bridge vanished and there was no trace of where it had been, not even the gossamer thread was there. All they could see or hear was a faint whimpering, and that no doubt was the Snake King bewailing the loss of his servants.

Happy and triumphant, Jacob led his company of girls back to the village and their parents. He and Margaret got married soon afterwards and they lived happily for the rest of their lives; but what happened to the Snake King and whether he was ever released, no one knows.

XI

# The Three Musicians

ONCE three young musicians went wandering in foreign lands. One played the violin, another the clarinet and the third the flute. It happened that they had studied music together under the same master and so had become friends. Their studies ended, they had decided that they would go off together to see the world and seek their fortunes.

They wandered along the highways and byways, playing their music at weddings and dances and on holidays in the villages and towns through which they passed. They were a young and merry trio, and they played so well that their music won them much applause and money enough for their needs.

One day found them in a small town where they agreed to play at a big wedding. The guests were gay and the three musicians played and played, till they could play no more, but had to stop and rest. They were given food to eat and wine to drink and people came up and talked with them. Many were the strange and curious things they heard, but perhaps the strangest of all was that they were told of a nearby castle. Some said it contained the loveliest treasures imaginable and was stocked with wines and fine foods enough to make anyone's mouth water, and yet nobody lived there; others spoke of a horrible ghost that was supposed to haunt it and that played mischievous tricks on any who ventured inside. Many who had gone in had come out black and blue and never even caught so much as a glimpse of any treasure, still less of the person who gave them their beating. This and much besides, the musicians heard about the castle and it made them most curious. So much so that, instead of going to bed, they stayed up for hours talking and discussing whether they should not have a look at this mysterious castle, perhaps even venture inside and have a try to find the treasure. In the end they decided that they must try to solve the mystery of the castle: each in turn, beginning with the eldest, was to go in alone and see what he could accomplish; each should have a whole day in which to make his attempt. That decided, they went to bed.

The violinist was the eldest. Gaily he set off on his way to the castle, which was only just outside the little town. Soon he came to some big gates that stood open and walked through them and on up a neglected drive. Rounding a bend he came to the castle itself. Its great door stood open, as though he were expected, so he stepped inside. The moment he was across the threshold, the heavy door banged shut and a thick bolt shot into place, and yet there was not a soul to be seen.

The musician's blood ran cold and his hair rose up on end. However, there was no going back now and no point in staying where he was, so, thinking of the treasure he hoped to find, the gold and precious things that were to make his fortune, he set off to explore the castle. Upstairs and downstairs he went, along corridors and into rooms all most magnificently furnished

## THE THREE MUSICIANS

and all clean, dusted and tidy. Yet there was not a sound to be heard, not a soul to be seen. The whole magnificent castle was silent as the grave.

Down in the basement was the kitchen, and there he found the loveliest dishes set out ready, and in the cellars were stacks of bottles of wine piled high and long rows of glass jars with bottled fruits and preserves of every kind.

The kitchen was clean and tidy; every pot and every pan bright and gleaming, and in the great hearth there burned a fire. As the young musician gazed at it, an invisible hand set a gridiron over the coals and a piece of the choicest venison came soaring out of the storeroom and settled on the grill. Other invisible hands were preparing all sorts of other dishes: glorious pasties and lovely pastries, tarts and cakes and pies. The young man wandered on and came back into one of the loveliest rooms, and there again invisible hands laid a table with a snow-white cloth and the finest silver, and set on it magnificent dishes filled with lovely things to eat.

First the young man took out his violin and played some of the loveliest melodies he knew, then, without hesitating, he sat down at the table and began to eat. It was not long before a door opened and in walked a little man only three feet high. He wore a scarlet coat, had a wizened face and grey beard that reached to the silver buckles on his shoes. Without saying a word, the little man walked across to the table, sat down and began to eat. Then the invisible hands served the roast of venison, that the musician had seen and smelt in the kitchen. The musician took the dish and presented it to the little man, so that he should help himself first. The

little man smiled his thanks and speared a large piece
on his fork, but just as that moment he nodded and the

The little man began to belabour the musician.

piece of meat fell from his fork to the ground. Respectfully the musician bent down to pick it up, and in a flash the little man was astride his back and had clamped one hand over his mouth. Thereupon the little man began to belabour the musician. In fact it looked as though he were trying to kill him. The poor musician began to run, and the old man on his back pummelled and pounded him all through the rooms and along the corridors and down the stairs, until they came to the great door which opened to let them out.

Once outside the poor musician found himself free. The little old man no longer sat astride his back. So, he heaved a great sigh of relief and, puffing and panting, limped off groaning with pain, back to the house where his companions were waiting for him.

Night had already fallen and by the time the violinist reached the house, the other two were already in bed and asleep, so he got into bed too. The next morning his companions were very surprised to see him calmly asleep in bed. They woke him up and began questioning him, demanding him to tell them all about it. The violinist scratched his head and glowered at them and all he would say was:

"Go and see for yourselves! It's a very ticklish business."

It was now the turn of the one who played the clarinet, and he set off for the castle as soon as he was dressed and ready. He found everything as the violinist had. He was given the loveliest meal and received the drubbing, so that when he woke up the next morning he ached all over. All he would say in answer to the others' questions was:

"You get a hearty reception there, and they certainly know how to beat time."

The third musician, the one who played the flute,

was not to be put off. He had plenty of courage and he was determined to go and, in his turn, try to solve the riddle of the mysterious castle. The flautist was the smartest of the three. Quite unafraid, he roamed all over the castle and he could not help thinking how lovely it would be to own such a magnificent place. He too came to the kitchen and saw all the dishes and glorious food, and he too found a table laid for two in one of the splendid rooms.

For a long time the third musician wandered about the castle singing and in the best of spirits, then, feeling hungry, he sat down at the table, blew his flute and began eating the glorious food that invisible hands brought from the kitchen. Again the door opened and the little man with the wizened face and grey beard came in and sat down beside his guest without saying a word. The musician was quite undaunted. He began conversing with the little man as though he knew him well and had met him a hundred times before. The little man, however, was not very talkative. Again venison was served, and again the little man deliberately let his piece drop. Good-naturedly, the flautist made to pick it up for him, but noticing that the little man was about to jump on his back, he turned round quickly, seized the man, shook him and pulled his beard so hard that it came off. The old man collapsed and fell groaning to the ground.

With the beard in his hand, the young man felt possessed of quite extraordinary strength, and, when he looked round, he saw lots of wonderful things that he had not noticed before. Meanwhile the little man lay on the ground, as though he were dying, groaning and whimpering:

"Give me, oh please, give me back my beard. I promise you that I'll take all the spells off, so that you will be rich and happy."

But the flautist was clever and said:

"Very well, you shall have your beard back, but first you must tell me everything; otherwise you are just a rogue."

So the little man was forced to make good his first promise, though he had not wanted to do that, but had hoped to get his beard back by cunning and then give nothing in return. The young musician followed him down dark passages and horrible gullies cut through rock, until at length they came into open country. This seemed to belong to a different world, for it was far lovelier than anything is here. They came to a river that foamed as it swirled along and looked quite impossible to cross; but the little man produced a wand from a pocket inside his coat and with it struck the water, and at once the waters halted and left the river bed free, so that they were able to walk across dryshod.

It was lovelier still on the other side of the river. They went along leafy walks and everywhere they saw all sorts of beautiful flowers; birds with feathers of silver and gold sang wonderful songs, and gleaming glistening beetles and gorgeous butterflies flitted and darted round them. Sweet little animals scampered in the hedges and bushes. The sky above was not blue, but a golden gleam. The stars were bigger than ours and moved about the heavens as though dancing some dance.

The young musician was amazed. He was even more amazed when the wizened old man led him into another building far more magnificent than the magic castle in which he had just been. Here too a deathly silence reigned in all the rooms and passages. They passed through a number of rooms and so came to one that was all hung with curtains, and in the middle of it stood a four-poster bed with the curtains drawn and above it hung a splendid birdcage in which a bird sang, sending the loveliest trills ringing through the silence. The little man pulled the curtains aside and beckoned to the young musician to approach. Going up close, the young man saw a lovely girl lying asleep, her head resting on soft silken pillows that were richly fringed with golden tassels. The girl was as beautiful as the dawn. She wore a white gown and her golden hair lay in long tresses across her shoulders. On her head she had a crown set with glistening diamonds, yet she lay in the grip of a deep and death-like sleep, and no noise seemed able to wake her. Then the little man said to the young musician:

"This sleeping girl, you see, is a high-born princess. This beautiful land and this magnificent castle are hers but for centuries she has been sleeping a sound and magic sleep; for hundreds of years no human being has found the way here. Only I have gone each day from here to my castle in order to eat there and to regale greedy humans with a sound drubbing. I am the guardian of this sleeping beauty and must take care to see that no stranger enters. That is why I have this long beard. It possesses such enormous power that I have been able to preserve this spell for hundreds of years. Now that my beard has been torn out, I am powerless and must give up this great happiness. So, now you must hurry up and complete what you have begun and free the princess. Take the bird from the cage hanging over the princess's bed. Once that bird sang her to sleep and ever since it has kept on singing just that one song; take it from the cage, kill it, cut out its little heart, burn this to ashes in the glowing embers of the hearth and sprinkle the powder on the princess's tongue. She will at once awake and will give you, her rescuer, her heart and her hand and endow you with her lands and castle and all its treasures."

Having said that, the little man with the wizened face sank down exhausted. The young man did not hesitate, but at once set about doing what had to be done in order to free the princess. Quickly and neatly he did all the things the dwarf had said, and before very long the powder was ready. A few minutes after he had sprinkled this powder on the princess's lips and tongue, she smiled and opened her eyes. Then she rose from her couch and took the young man's hand and began to thank him for freeing her from the magic spell. Her lands and castle were to be his, she said, and if he cared, her hand as well.

As she said that a rumble of thunder echoed through the castle, and all at once you could hear steps and voices on the stairs and all the rooms were full of people. Servants and ladies-in-waiting crowded into the room where the princess and her rescuer were. Everyone was happy and smiling, glad to be restored to life, and quickly they got to work in the kitchen and cellar, in the rooms and corridors; glad to be busy again.

Meanwhile the grey dwarf had recovered, and he now energetically demanded that his beard be given back to him. In his wicked mind he was still hoping to be able to play a trick on the happy princess and her rescuer. For once the beard was back on his chin, he would have all his former powers again and would be able to impose his will on any mortal. But the flute player was a smart young fellow and he was still suspicious of the wicked old man, so he said:

"You can have your beard back; you shall have it as a parting present, first allow me and the princess to accompany you part of the way."

The little man could scarcely refuse to agree, so they walked off back along the way the young musician and the dwarf had come, along the leafy walks and past the beds of wonderful flowers, until at length they came to the river that ran as deep and as fiercely as ever. This great river ran for miles and miles round the princess's lands and formed their boundary. Nowhere was there a bridge nor any boat to be had that could have taken people across, and even the strongest swimmer could never have reached the other side through those wildly tossing waters.

Then the young musician spoke to the dwarf and said:

"Give me your wand, so that this time I may part the waters for you."

The dwarf had to do what the other told him, but to himself he said: "Just you wait till I reach the other side and get my beard back, then I shall have you both in my power and you will not be able to go back."

But the dwarf's evil plan was not to succeed. The young musician struck the water with the wand and at once the waters divided, part standing still, while the rest flowed on leaving the river-bed bare. The dwarf went first and walked quickly across. The moment he was up on the other bank, the waters closed again and the river flowed on, roaring, as before. The young musician and the princess had stayed on the bank that was on the princess's land. Keeping the wand that alone could divide the waters, the young man hurled the dwarf's beard with all his strength. It just reached the other side. The dwarf picked it up and put it on, but bereft of his magic wand he was unable to cross the river and thus never again could he set foot on the princess's land.

The happy young musician walked back to the castle with the princess. Soon they were married and lived happily ever afterwards. The musician's companions waited for him in vain, and when they realized that he was not coming back, they went on their way in search of their fortunes.

## XII

# The Nine Hills of Rambin

IN the western part of the island of Ruegen, in the flat land not far from the village of Rambin, are nine little hillocks or mounds known as the Nine Hills of Rambin. These came into being in the days of the giants, and since the giants died, the elves have used them.

The giant who made the Nine Hills was called Balderich. It always annoyed him that he lived on an island and had to wade through the sea whenever he wanted to go to Pomerania, so one day he had a huge apron made, tied it round his waist and filled it with earth with which he intended to build a causeway between the island and the mainland. When he came to Rodenkirchen a hole tore in the apron and some of the earth trickled down and made the Nine Hills of Rambin. The giant noticed this, mended the hole and went on his way.

These nine little hills are now used by the elves who live underground there, and at night they come up and dance in the bushes and fields in the moonlight. Their favourite times for doing this are in the lovely, fine nights of summer, and in the spring, when all the trees are blossoming. The elves have many boys and girls in their service, but they do not let these come up from below, but keep them underground, for most of them the dwarfs have stolen or got hold of by some lucky chance, and they are afraid of their running away. In the old days many children who went to the Nine Hills to play early in the morning, or who stayed there late in the evening, used to let themselves be enticed by the sweet music and songs that came from the bushes and ran there to listen, thinking it was little songbirds singing, and then the elves captured them and took them to their dwellings deep underground, where they had to wait on the elves as their servants. But now that people know what can happen, they are careful, and children never go there. Even so, whenever some innocent child disappears, people say that the elves have taken it, and often indeed they are right and the little brown people have captured it by their arts, and then the poor child has to stay underground and serve the elves and never come home again. However, it is an age-old law of those who live underground, that once every fifty years they must let up into the light all whom they may have caught. And another good thing for those poor captives who have to serve the little brown elves is that their years underground are not reckoned as part of their lives and that no one can become more than twenty years old there below, even when he has to spend the full fifty years in the elves' service. That is why all who come out are young and handsome. Also, most people who have once served the brown elves have luck during the rest of their lives above ground; either because their stay underground has made them clever and ingenious, or, as some people say, because the little brown people, who are invisible, help them at their work and bring them gold and silver.

The elves who live in seven of the Nine Hills of Rambin are brown elves, who are not bad or nasty in any way; and in the other two hills live white elves who are the friendliest and handsomest of all the little people and do only good. There are also black elves who are expert at working iron and clever at many other things, but also magicians and sorcerers, full of trickery and guile, and them you cannot trust. However, none of these lived at Rambin.

Now at Rambin, once long ago, there lived a hardworking man called Jacob Dietrich who had a son, Johann, who used to go with the other boys to help old Claus herd the villagers' cows which used to graze near the Nine Hills. Old Claus knew a great deal about the peoples who lived underground, and the old, old days when the giants had died out and the elves came to the hills in their stead. Johann loved listening to old Claus and drank it all in. Thus it was that he learned how to become master of the little people and not their servant, for whoever is clever enough, or lucky enough to find or get hold of the cap of an elf can safely go to their homes underground, since as long as he keeps the cap, the elves can do nothing to him, nor give him orders, but must obey him and do as he says, and the one to whom the cap belonged must be his servant and do his bidding.

One year, on Midsummer's Day, when the night was shortest, Johann slipped away from his house as soon as it was dark and climbed to the top of the tallest of the Nine Hills where the elves had their favourite dancing-floor, and there he lay down and waited. He was a little bit afraid, as you will understand, and his heart thumped, but he lay on from ten till midnight. And when midnight sounded, from inside the hill came a tinkling and a sound of singing, and soon there was whispering and whistles and rustlings all around where Johann lay. So the little people danced, while others played, and they romped in the moonlight, but Johann could not see them, for the caps that elves wear make them invisible.

As Johann lay there pretending to be asleep, three elves came running along, throwing their caps into the air and catching them again. Then one of them seized the other's cap from his hand and threw it from him. It landed on Johann's head. Johann felt it, seized hold of it and leaped to his feet, and, oh, wonder of wonders, he could now see the throng of little people. They were invisible no longer. The three elves came stealing up to try and snatch the cap, but Johann held on to it, and, being a giant compared with the elves, he realized that they could not do anything by force. Then the one whose cap it was came up humbly and begged for his cap back again, but Johann said: "No, I have your cap and I shall keep it. I want to go back with you and see how you live down there and you must be my servant." The poor elf had to agree. There was no getting out of it.

Johann at once put him to the test and told him to bring him food and drink. The elf sped away and was back in a trice with a bottle of wine, bread and rare fruits. Johann ate and drank and watched the dancing of the elves, and enjoyed himself immensely.

As the cocks in the village crowed for the third time and the first shafts of white light appeared in the east, a rustle passed through the bushes and flowers and grasses, and the hill-top lifted and a gleaming spike of glass appeared; whoever wished to descend stepped on to this when it opened, and he slid slowly down into a large silver barrel that had room for at least a thousand such little people. Into this Johann also slid with his servant, and they all cried out to him and begged him to be careful with his feet. And Johann was very careful. Then slowly the silver barrel began to descend, hanging on silver chains. The walls of the shaft shimmered and glowed as though set with pearls and diamonds, and there was the sound of the loveliest music which sent Johann into a deep sleep.

Johann must have slept a long time, for when he woke up, he found himself in the softest and loveliest bed in a sweet little room, and beside his bed stood his brown elf servant, waving a fly switch to keep the flies away. No sooner did the elf see his eyes open than he fetched water and towel for Johann to wash, and brought new clothes of brown silk for him to wear. As soon as he was dressed, his elfin servant sped away to return with a golden tray on which stood a bottle of wine, a jug of milk, fine white bread, fruit and other lovely things.

When Johann had finished breakfast, his servant opened the door of a little cupboard in the wall and, looking in, Johann saw a whole service of golden and silver cups and plates, baskets full of golden ducats, boxes of jewels and precious stones. There were lovely books and pictures as well, and, seeing all this, Johann announced that he would not go out that morning, but would spend it investigating the contents of the cupboard.

At midday a bell rang and Johann's servant said: "Master, will you eat in private or with the great company?" "With the great company," Johann replied and his elf led him out and into the corridor. As they walked along Johann saw little men and women who seemed to come out of cracks in the rock, and he wondered where the bell was ringing and where the great company was. All at once the corridor widened out into an endless, huge room with a great vaulted roof studded with the diamonds and other jewels that acted as the elves' lamps and provided their light. At the same moment, a vast multitude of neatly-dressed little women came pouring through numbers of wide-opened doors, and in many places the floor opened and tables rose up laden with the finest of food and drink and chairs appeared beside them and on these the elves seated themselves. Then the head elves came up and conducted Johann to the high table and made him sit in the seat of honour. There was the loveliest music that seemed to come from the air, in which brightly-coloured birds flew about singing. These were not live birds, but artificial ones so cleverly made that they both sang and flew. Johann was full of wonder and admiration for the elves.

The servants who waited at table, strewed flowers and sprinkled essence of roses and other scents, and bore round the golden trays and silver baskets, were all mortals, children whom inquisitiveness or mischance had led into the hands of the elves. They wore snow-white uniforms with glass shoes, so that they could be heard wherever they went, and little blue caps and silver belts round their waists. Such was the dress of the servants. At first, seeing how they had to run about as they waited on the elves, Johann felt sorry for them, but then he noticed that they all had happy expressions and red cheeks, so he decided that they could not have a hard time of it—in fact probably better than he had had, helping to herd the village cows.

Dinner lasted a good two hours, then the head elf rang a bell and the tables and chairs sank back into the floor and disappeared, leaving Johann and the elves standing there. Then a second bell rang and, where the tables has been, rose green orange trees and palms and flowering shrubs and bushes in which other birds sat, and these sang even more beautifully than those that before had flown through the air, and they all sang in a chorus. Up by the roof was a niche in the wall in which sat a grey-haired man who conducted the birds. Then the old man, whom they called the ball-master, began to play dance tunes on a violin and the birds sang the same tune, and so the elves danced. The little elves, between whom Johann had sat, took him by the arm and made him dance too, and he thoroughly enjoyed himself.

At length the music stopped; the dance was ended and the merry elves dispersed back to their work and their pleasure. In the evening they assembled again to dine, and sometimes they danced after dinner as well, but at midnight they all went up out of the hill, especially on clear, starry nights or when they had anything special to do in the world of mortals. Johann, however, always went to bed and slept soundly and well in his room which was close by the place where the great dining hall came and went.

In all the years that he was there, Johann never saw one of the elves' own rooms, nor could he see how they came in and out of the rock in which they had their dwellings, so quickly did they move. He was told that each had his own little glass house deep in the rock, and that the whole hill was transparent and surrounded with glass, only his eyes could not see it.

The tallest of these elves was only three feet high, and the children were tiny indeed. They had friendly faces, light eyes and small hands and feet. No one knows whether they die or not; certainly no one has ever seen a dead elf. Some say that when they become old, they creep into a stone or a tree and become the sighs and creaks and other strange noises that you sometimes hear without being able to tell from where they come. Certainly many of the elves are well over two thousand years old, so it is no wonder that some of them are so wise and clever.

One great advantage the elves have—they do not need to work for their daily bread; for their food and drink comes of itself in some magic way; there is always bread, wine and meat on their tables. Nor do you ever see corn growing or cattle grazing in their underground realm, but only fruit trees and flowers and things to give pleasure. The elves understand how to be happy and enjoy themselves, yet you must not think that they just eat, dance and amuse themselves, for though they dance and frolic in the moonlight, they can also go to the houses of mortals and put presents in the children's beds or help those who are in trouble. Often elves are there, invisibly watching over children when their parents are busy. Elves frighten lazy or dishonest workers; they lead thieves astray in the night and, as will-o'-the-wisps, entice others into swamps and marshes; in fact they can do good in many ways.

One day, when Johann had been several months with the elves, he was out for a walk with his servant in the evening twilight when he saw something white slip into a crystal rock and disappear. Thinking it must be one of the elves, he asked his servant if there were elves who dressed in white, like the servants, instead of the normal brown. The servant replied: "Yes, but not many. They never appear at dances, nor at the great dinners, except once a year for the birthday banquet of the mountain king who lives several thousand miles beneath here. That is why you have never seen them. They are the oldest of us, some of them several thousand years old, and they can tell about the beginning of the world and the origin of things. They are known as the Wise Ones. They keep very much to themselves and only come out of their rooms to teach our children and servant children in the schools."

"What, is there a school here?" exclaimed Johann. "I have always wanted to go to school. Can I go here?"

"Indeed you can," replied the elf. "You are the master here and only have to say. Would you like to go to an elf school or to the servant school? Or you could have one of the Wise Ones come to your room."

"No," said Johann, "I want to go to the servant children's school and learn with mortals. I might not be able to keep up with you elves."

The very next morning Johann went to school, and he liked it so much that after that he never missed a day. Before long he much preferred learning to the

the dances and other entertainments of the elves, and also he enjoyed the company of the servant children who were mortals like he. He became particularly fond of one sweet little fair-haired girl called Lisbeth, who happened to come from the same village of Rambin. She and some other children had been playing on one of the Nine Hills, and Lisbeth had fallen asleep there. The other children had gone away without noticing her, and when she woke up, it was after midnight and she was in the midst of the elfin dance.

The years passed and Johann never gave a thought to the world above. He became eighteen and Lisbeth sixteen, and what had been a childish friendship ripened into true love. Johann and Lisbeth took to going for long walks by themselves, and they preferred being alone to the company of others. One night, when they were out for a walk and had forgotten time and everything else but themselves, they suddenly heard the sound of cocks crowing, and the strangest feeling came over Lisbeth. She clung to Johann and confessed to him that she had never been really happy with the elves till she found Johann there, and though the elves treated them all so well and they had an easy time, there being no really hard or dirty work in the elves' world, she wished she were back in the world of ordinary people and could see her father and mother, whom she dearly loved. Also, she said, there was no church in the world of the elves, and so she and Johann could never be married, and she loved him dearly and wanted to be his wife, so they must try to get away.

The sound of the cocks' crowing also affected Johann

strangely, and he too found himself longing for the world of mortals, and though he could go back when he liked, Lisbeth was bound by strict laws and must wait till her years were up, but without Lisbeth Johann was determined not to go, yet he could think of no way of freeing her. They were sad as they parted that night.

In the morning, Johann sent for the six head elves and asked them to let him go and take Lisbeth with him, but they said "No". It was a strict rule that none of the servants must leave before their time was up, and fond though they had become of Johann, they could not do this for him. Johann was angry and ordered them to release Lisbeth. Again they refused.

The next day Johann sent for the head elves again and spoke to them very sternly, but still they refused to release Lisbeth. After that, Johann sent for their wives and daughters and made them all work hard from early till late, but still they would not give in. He did that for six days till he could bear the sight no longer.

One day as Johann was walking sadly along he took to throwing stones. One stone, larger than the rest, split as it fell and out rolled what was to prove Johann's salvation. This was a toad which had lived in that stone perhaps since the creation of the world. Johann's heart leapt for joy when he saw it. The toad hopped away and Johann ran after it and caught it and put it in his pocket and ran back as fast as he could to his room, where he put the toad in a silver dish to prevent its escaping. Johann was so overjoyed that he behaved as though he were crazy and talked aloud to himself, saying "Now I have them. Now I shall get my Lisbeth." Then he picked up the silver dish and said to the toad, "Now let's see if you really work." and, going out with the dish, he walked towards a couple of elves who were out for a stroll. As he drew near, the two elves fell to the ground, screaming and moaning most pitiably. The moment he saw, it, Johann turned and ran home like the wind. When he got to his room, he called his servant and told him to fetch Lisbeth.

When Lisbeth came she was surprised to see Johann gay and happy, for he had seldom been anything but sad the last six months. And Johann cried out: "Now Lisbeth darling, now you are mine. Now I shall take you with me. The day after tomorrow we go." Poor Lisbeth could not understand and was worried until Johann showed her the toad in its silver dish and explained how the elves cannot stand either the sight or smell of a toad, which cause them the most appalling pain, so that you can force them to anything if you have a toad, as you can with any foul smell, for there is nothing foul or nasty in all the world of the elves.

The next morning Johann told his servant to send for the head elves with their wives and daughters, and when the were all assembled, Johann spoke to them, reproaching them for not doing things when he asked them nicely, nor even when he bullied them a little, so that now he was forced to be very hard and cruel, but he would give them one minute in which to agree to release Lisbeth.

The head elves were very surprised and wondered what new trick Johann could have thought of, but, now knowing, they of course said "No", and they smiled to themselves as they said it. Then Johann said: "Very well, then!" and he ran to the place a hundred yards away where he had hidden the dish with the toad under a bush. Then he began his walk back.

He had only taken a few paces when the elves all fell to the ground and began to whimper and moan and contort themselves as though in dreadful pain. They then cried out: "Stop, stop, we know that you have a toad and that we cannot escape. Take the foul thing away and we will do whatever you say." So Johann let them have a few seconds' more torment and then removed the silver dish.

Johann then gave his orders: that night, between twelve and one, he and Lisbeth would leave, taking with them three waggons laden with gold and silver and precious stones. Though he could have taken everything the elves possessed, he intended to be reasonable, he told them. Also all the things in Johann's room were to go with him. They were to prepare a coach with six black horses to drive Johann and Lisbeth home, and at the same time all the servants who had been there so long that, if they had remained on earth, they would have been twenty or older, were to be released and given as much gold and silver as would enable them to live well for the rest of their lives.

The six head elves had to agree to all this and set about making the preparations. When all the servants who were to be released and all the waggons and precious things had been taken up to the earth above, Johann and Lisbeth said goodbye to the elves and got into the silver barrel and were taken up in their turn. It was one o'clock in the morning as they stepped out on to the top of the same one of the Nine Hills from which Johann had descended. Stepping out, Johann took his brown cap and, swinging it thrice round his head, flung it from him. From that moment he was unable to see the elves, only the green hills and familiar trees and bushes; but the waggons were there with their precious loads, and the coach too.

A lark soared into the sky and the sun rose. Johann ordered the coach, waggons and the released servants into a procession, mounted the coach where Lisbeth already sat, and so they drove to Rambin.

At the sound of the hooves and wheels, windows opened and people came out into the street in their night things. Never had such elegant people or such fine waggons been seen in Rambin. You can imagine how surprised Johann's parents were when a smart, richly dressed young man took them in his arms and said that he was their son. And Lisbeth's old parents did not recognize her either, but she kissed them and told them who she was and they wept tears of joy.

Eight days later Johann and Lisbeth were married, and they lived most happily ever after.

# XIII

# The Cobbler's Two Sons

ONE day a cobbler went fishing and caught three carp, each of which weighed ten pounds. As he was carrying his heavy load home, he dropped one of the carp, but, glad to be relieved of its weight, he walked on. The carp, on the ground, called out "Stop". Then the cobbler turned round and said: "I don't want a fish that can shout", and walked on. A little while later he dropped another of the fish, and this too called out "Stop", only to be told that the cobbler did not want a fish that could talk. When the same thing happened with the third fish, it called back again "If you take me home, it will bring you luck."

"What luck can you bring me, you poor fish?" asked the cobbler.

"Just take me home and do what I say and you'll see," said the carp.

The cobbler picked up the carp and walked on. When they reached home, the fish said: "If you cut my belly open, you will find a lump of gold on one side and a stone on the other. Bury these near a tree. Give my brains to your wife to eat and she will present you with two little golden-haired boys. Give my head to your horse and he will bring you two colts with golden manes. Give my tail to your dog and he will bring you two golden-coloured puppies."

The cobbler then picked up the fish, did as it had told him and all that it had said came true: he found a lump of gold on one side of its belly and a stone on the other; his wife presented him with two boys, his horse brought him two colts and his dog two puppies.

When the boys grew bigger, the cobbler, who was now quite well-off thanks to the gold, arranged for his sons to go to school. Sometime later, he met the schoolmaster, and the schoolmaster asked him why his sons never came to school. When he got back home, the cobbler asked his two boys what the schoolmaster had meant, and where they went instead of to the schoolmaster's school. The boys replied that they did not dare tell him till they were twelve years old. However, they were very hard-working and wherever they went, it seemed to be a good school, for they knew more and more every day. Then their twelfth birthday arrived and they confessed to their father that they had been going to school at the tree where he had buried the stone.

The two boys now wanted to leave home and go off into the world, so they asked their father to give them each one of the horses and one of the dogs, but their father would not hear of it. Not long after this, however, the two boys got up in the middle of the night; each took one of the horses with golden manes and calling to the golden-coloured dogs they rode off together.

When they had ridden some distance one of them, Hans, said to the other, Carl: "Listen, Carl, we two always see alike and that won't do, so let us now separate. I'll climb this tall oak and see if I can discover two roads and we'll each take one."

Hans climbed the tree, and in the distance he saw a light. When he came down again, he said: "I am going this way; you go that. Before we go, let us each fasten a rose to this oak. If one comes back and finds the other's rose faded, he will know that the other is ill; but if the rose is quite withered, that will mean that the other is dead. In this way we shall each know how the other has fared." So then the two separated and went different ways.

After some time Hans came to an inn and as he sat there, he asked the innkeeper: "What news?"

"Not much news," said the innkeeper, "except that the king is going to hold a fencing-match at which anyone who likes can challenge his three daughters' suitors. If anyone can defeat one of them, he is to have that princess for his wife."

"Well," said Hans to himself, "perhaps I could have a try. I am not a bad swordsman." Then he borrowed a ragged coat from the manservant of the inn and walked off to the fencing-school leaving his horse and dog at the inn.

When Hans reached the fencing-school, the match had already begun and the elder daughter's suitor had just defeated the last of those who had challenged him. "For the last time," said the herald: "Does anyone else challenge the suitor?" Then Hans stepped forward. The suitor laughed and said: "I'll soon finish off this fellow." But Hans happened to have a quicker eye than the suitor, and he ran him through with his sword.

## THE COBBLER'S TWO SONS

When the princess saw that the ragged and unknown young man had defeated her suitor and should now be her husband, she turned to her father and said: "I will not have him!" So the king asked Hans if he would take five hundred gulden instead of marrying the princess. "Why not," said Hans. "Indeed, I will. There are other ladies here." So he pocketed the money.

Then the suitor of the second princess entered the lists, and again no one could defeat him. In the end only Hans had not measured his skill against his, and, as Hans stepped forward, the suitor gazed at him contemptuously. Hans' answer was to cut his arm off with one slash of his sword. The younger princess did not like the idea of having Hans for a husband any more than her sister had, so Hans received another five hundred gulden which he pocketed, gaily saying: "There are others here!"

Then the suitor of the third and youngest princess came into the lists. He too, defeated all his opponents until only Hans was left, and this time the quick-eyed Hans cut off his foot. The last and youngest princess, however, was not so sure as her sisters about Hans. In fact, she thought his golden hair and fresh, open face rather nice and handsome, and she told him that he must go up to the castle-yard and she would look down from a window and tell him whether or not she would have him for her husband.

Hans went up to the great courtyard and, as she had promised, the princess looked out, and then she told him that she would marry him. Then some courtiers came out and they wanted to give Hans fine clothes, for they thought him poor and ragged, but Hans asked to be allowed to absent himself for a short while and hurried back to the inn where he put on his own fine clothes, mounted his horse and with his dog trotting beside, rode back to the castle. How astonished everyone was when they saw the young princess's future husband ride up on a horse with a golden mane, and running beside it a golden-haired dog, while the young man's own hair glistened like gold in the sunlight. The two elder sisters were not only astonished but horribly envious, especially the eldest.

Hans and the young princess were married and lived very happily for several weeks. But the eldest sister could not get over her envy and kept trying to devise some way of getting rid of Hans. In the end she went to a witch who lived outside the city altogether, in the great forest, and asked her if she could not help her get rid of Hans. "Give me three hundred gulden," said the witch, "and arrange for a hunt which must bring him through this part of the forest, and I will get rid of him for you and no one will ever see him again." The princess was delighted, gave the witch the money and went home to arrange the hunt.

The day for the hunt arrived. The witch climbed into a tall tree in a remote part of the forest and sat there. Presently Hans came riding along, and seeing the old woman on her lofty perch, he called to her: "What are you doing up there? Come down!" "Ah, my lord," the cunning old woman answered, "I dare not, your little dog might bite me. Take this rod which I will throw down to you and switch about you to keep your little dog out of the way." Hans caught the rod she threw down and brandished it behind him. The moment he did so he vanished and with him his horse and his dog.

The news spread like wildfire and everyone mourned the young princess's handsome husband.

One day shortly after this Hans' brother Carl came back to the tall oak where the two brothers had parted. To his grief he saw that Hans' rose had withered. "Poor Hans," he thought. "I see that you must be dead, but at least I shall find out where you died and how it happened." So he set off down the same road that Hans had taken when they parted.

Carl rode on till he came to the city; there he found the windows of all the houses draped with black and everyone dressed in deep mourning. He came to the inn, and going inside, asked what disaster had befallen the city. "Why," said the innkeeper, "don't you know? Do you mean to say that you have not heard how our young princess's husband has disappeared? But, of course, you are joking, for, I can see now, you are he." That told Carl all he needed to know, for he and his brother were remarkably like each other, so the princess's husband must have been his brother Hans. While the innkeeper spread the news of Hans' return, Carl went up to the castle, where he was received with great joy. Even the young princess was overjoyed, for she too mistook him for Hans, until she asked him why he looked so sad and he told her that he was not Hans, but his brother and that he had come to find out what had happened to him.

Meanwhile the eldest princess in a great fury had rushed to the witch in the forest and was demanding that the witch pay back the three hundred gulden she had been given for making Hans disappear.

"Come down at once," he cried in a furious voice, "or I will shoot you."

## THE COBBLER'S TWO SONS

"You fool," said the witch, when she had heard the angry princess's story, "that is not your sister's husband, but his brother. Go back and arrange for another hunt and I'll soon get rid of him too." And this the horrible eldest sister was able to do, as she had on the first occasion. And still everybody else, except the youngest princess, thought that Carl was his brother.

The day for the hunt came, and before very long the chase brought Carl to the very place where his brother had vanished, and there he saw the old witch who was again perched up in her tall tree. He called to the old woman to come down, and again she answered: "My lord, I am afraid; your little dog might bite me." This time, however, she got a different answer. Realizing that she must be a witch and have caused his brother's disappearance, Carl became very angry indeed. "Come down at once," he cried in a furious voice, "or I will shoot you. You have cast a spell on my brother, and if you do not this minute bring him back to life, you are a dead woman." Now the old witch was really frightened and she promised that she would bring Hans back to life as soon as she reached the ground. So she climbed down out of the tree, and as soon as her feet were on the mossy ground at the foot of the tree, she took her rod and hit the earth with it three times. No sooner had she done that than there, lying in front of them were Hans, his horse and his dog, but they were lifeless. Then the old witch took her rod again and touched each of them with it, and all three were restored to life.

You can imagine how delighted the brothers were to see each other. They embraced, and then they set upon the old witch to punish her and tore her to pieces. After that they rode back to the city. The youngest princess was overjoyed to see Hans alive and well, and all the people rejoiced.

When, in the fullness of time, Hans became King, Carl was made Viceroy, and for all I know, they may still be living yet.

# XIV

# The Three White Doves

HANSEL lived with his mother until he was nineteen years old, when he set out to seek his fortune.

Somehow he lost his way going through a forest, and seeing a light through the trees, he came to a tumbledown cottage where a very ugly and very old man was living. But the old man was kind enough to Hansel and said that he could stay and work for him, but he must work for a year and three days or else bad luck would overtake him. Hansel agreed to work for the old man, and when the year and three days was up, his master said: "You have served me so faithfully and well that you can take as much gold away with you as you can carry, also this white dove, but you must obey these instructions. When you reach home you must build a castle there and pull out three feathers from the dove. It will then be turned into a beautiful maiden, who will become your wife. But hide the three feathers from her carefully, for if she ever finds them, disaster will come to you."

Hansel thanked the old man for his gifts and advice,

and set out for home. When he reached his home, he did build a castle, and he did pull three feathers from the white dove, and it did turn into a lovely maiden whom he married, all exactly as the ugly old man had said. For three years Hansel and his bride were very happy, but then one day when he was out hunting his wife and his mother were sitting sewing and talking together. "I don't think there is any woman in the world so beautiful as you," said Hansel's mother. "Oh, but if I only had the feathers my husband has hidden, I should be much more beautiful," sighed Hansel's wife. This remark made Hansel's mother most curious and knowing where he kept the feathers, she took them and gave them to the girl. In a moment she had stuck the feathers into her body and turned back into the white dove. When Hansel came home, she thanked him for his kindness to her and flew out of the window and away.

Hansel was terribly sad to lose the sweet wife of whom he was so fond, and he decided to go to the ugly old man in the forest and beg for his advice and help.

All the old man could do was to send Hansel to his brother, who lived far, far away and was the ruler of all the birds and beasts. He told a dwarf to show Hansel the way, and after a long and tiring journey they came to the old man's brother, who was even older and more hideous, but just as willing to help Hansel as his brother had been. "I do not know where you can seek the white dove," growled the old man, "but I will ask all the creatures under my command."

He took a little whistle and blew through it and in a moment the whole place was seething with animals and birds who cried: "What are our ruler's commands?" The old man asked them about the white dove, but they all fell silent and shook their heads. "None of my subjects know," said the old man, "so you must go to my elder brother, who is the ruler of all the dwarfs, giants and witches; perhaps he will be able to help you." So saying he told a giant eagle to carry Hansel to his brother. Hansel mounted the eagle and by that evening they had arrived at the home of the ruler of all dwarfs, giants and witches. This brother was an enormous man. He wore a wreath of oak branches in his hair and carried a whole fir tree in his massive hand.

Hansel felt sure this giant of a man could help him to find his wife, so he asked him where he should search for the white dove. The giant struck the ground with his fir tree, and in a moment the whole place was seething with his subjects, who cried: "What are our ruler's commands?" The giant asked them about the white dove, but they also fell silent and shook their heads. The giant looked round and roared: "Where is Limper?" "Here! Here!" cried Limper, out of breath with running. "I have chased the white dove over three seas! She is with two others and I could not catch them, because they reached the palace in the middle of the sea where they dwell." "Good," replied the giant, "fly with this man to the palace of the three doves!" and turning to Hansel he whispered: "If Limper should ask you any question, you must only answer 'No'."

Hansel thanked the giant and climbed on to Limper's back and away they went through the air.

They flew for two days. Then, at last, they could see the shining roof of the doves' palace in the distance.

"Do you see the roof?" Limper asked. "No," answered Hansel, closing his eyes, for he had been warned to answer "no" or else Limper would let him fall. When they were even nearer, Limper asked again: "Do you see the palace?" And again Hansel answered "No". At last they were right above the roof, and again Limper asked: "Now do you see the roof?" "No," said Hansel, and Limper growled, "Fool, you must be blind!" and he swooped down to the palace and left Hansel there.

Inside the palace were the three white doves. They were doves in the morning and evening, but turned into humans for the rest of the day. Hansel's wife at once recognized him and said: "At last you have come to set me free!" But she could not tell him how to do so. He searched the palace rooms until he came to a locked door, and this he managed to break open. There in the middle of the room stood a table with three glasses of water upon it. Above the table hung a huge dragon, tied to the ceiling by his hands. He begged Hansel to give him a glass of water, promising to save his life in return. Hansel gave the water to the dragon, and when the dragon had drunk it, one of his hands was freed. Then he begged for the second glass of water, in return for which he promised again to save Hansel's life, and again Hansel gave him the drink, and so the dragon's second hand was freed. "Now give me the third glass," roared the dragon, "or I will kill you and eat you!" Hansel was so frightened that he handed him the glass of water which freed the dragon completely. It then flew through the palace chasing the doves and at last caught the one which was Hansel's wife. The other two doves reproached Hansel for setting the dragon free, and told him that he must now seek their three brothers who had been turned into horses. The youngest was in the palace stable, the second in the dragon's stable, and the eldest was in the stable of a bad and powerful old witch.

Hansel searched until he found the palace stables and spoke with the youngest horse, who told him that the dragon was out at that moment and if Hansel could manage to steal the dove and jump on his back, he would fly away with them. Hansel found the dove and they were just flying off, when, to their horror, the dragon returned, and seeing them escaping, he leaped onto another horse and flew after them and caught them up. Because he had promised to save Hansel's life when he gave him the drink of water, the dragon did not kill Hansel, although he was furiously angry. Hansel was in despair, but the horse urged him to have courage and to try and escape with the dove next time that the dragon was out. Once more they set out on their flight, and again the dragon returned before they had gone very far and caught them up. But although he was roaring with rage and snorting flames, he still kept his word and spared Hansel's life a second time, because of the promise he had made when the second glass of water was given him. "But," he bellowed, "if you steal my favourite dove a third time, then I shall tear you into little pieces."

Hansel begged the horse to think of some other way of rescuing the dove, and the horse told Hansel that he must go to the bad old witch and ask to be her servant for three days: "At the end of the time you must ask for the worst of her horses as payment, for the worst horse in her stable is my brother," he said.

Hansel set out, and on his way he saw a huge fly struggling in a spider's web. He felt sorry for it and set it free, and the fly thanked him and said: "If ever you are in great trouble, think of me and I will help you."

Hansel went on, and soon he came across a poor fox that had fallen into a pit. He hauled the fox out of the pit, and the fox said: "If ever you are in great trouble think of me, and I will help you."

Soon after that Hansel came to the sea and saw a huge crab kicking on its back in the sand; so he turned the crab the right way up, and it was so grateful that it called hundreds of its friends and relations together, and they built a bridge so that Hansel could cross over the sea.

The old witch was looking out from her castle and saw Hansel a long way off. She came out to meet him and asked, with a sly grin, if he would be her servant. Hansel agreed to serve her, and the old witch said: "The work only lasts for three days, and you will have nothing else to do but take my horses out to the pasture and watch over them while they graze. But if you lose even one of my horses, I shall cut off your head!" And she snarled, showing her yellow, pointed teeth.

The old witch gave Hansel a piece of bread to take out to the pasture for himself, and sent him forth with her herd of horses. Hansel felt terribly hungry, and although the old lean horse warned him not to eat the bread that the witch had given him, he could wait no longer, but ate a piece of the bread and at once fell sound asleep. When he awoke, all the horses had gone. He called and searched for them, but could not find any trace of them. Suddenly he remembered the fly that he had saved from the spider and thought of its offer of help. No sooner had he thought of it, than it appeared flying along ahead of all the horses who were galloping after it. Hansel was overjoyed. He thanked the fly and drove all the horses home. The old witch was waiting for him, and when she had counted the horses and found that none was missing, she was furious and, growling with rage, took up a stick and beat Hansel and her horses.

Next day Hansel took the horses out again, and again the witch gave him a piece of bread to eat. He threw the bread away, but after a little while he became so appallingly hungry that he went back and searched for it and picked it up and ate it. At once he fell asleep, and when he woke up the horses had vanished again. He was searching and crying with despair, when he suddenly remembered the fox. And at once the fox appeared with all the horses, and Hansel drove the whole herd home. When the old witch found that there were still no horses missing, she shrieked and beat them and Hansel more cruelly than ever.

The third and last morning came. The witch gave Hansel a large piece of bread and told him sternly that he must eat every crumb. But he crumbled it up and threw it away as soon as he was out of sight, yet in a short time he was feeling so ravenously hungry that he had to search the ground and ate all the crumbs of bread he could pick up. At once he fell asleep again, and when he woke up there was not a horse to be seen. They had dashed into the sea to hide, and Hansel wept, saying: "Now I have no one left to help me. The fly first found the horses and saved my life, then the fox, and the crab and his fellows have already helped me across the sea. Now the witch will kill me and all through my own foolishness!" But just as he mentioned the crab, the horses all came galloping back

"You shall have the finest horse in my stable," crooned the witch.

with water streaming from their sides. The crab and his friends had heard Hansel's lament and had sidled up and nipped all the horses' heels, so that they had to trot quickly out of their hiding place in the sea.

## THE THREE WHITE DOVES

With a light heart Hansel drove the herd home. He had finished his task and could claim his reward. The old witch looked at him with hungry flashing eyes. "You have served me well," she crooned in a per-

But Hansel chose the lean horse.

suasive voice, "you shall have the finest horse in my stable in payment for your services." But Hansel chose the lean horse and refused to take any other. Then the old witch, seeing him about to slip from her clutches, gave him the lean horse and another one, saying he could ride that one and spare the old lean horse by leading it. Hansel accepted her offer and mounted the good horse and led the other, but just as they were reaching the gates of the witch's castle, the old horse whispered: "Dismount quickly and jump on my back!" Hansel did so and the strong horse wheeled round snorting angrily, for if Hansel had stayed on its back, it had been going to rear up under the gateway and crush Hansel's head against the stones. Hansel now rode on without further mishap until he came to the palace of the three doves. The old horse told him to wait until the dragon fell asleep and then to steal the doves from him. Hansel crept into the palace and hid until the dragon fell asleep, then he took the doves and mounted the lean horse which suddenly grew and grew and grew until it was enormous. When the dragon woke up and found his doves gone, he rushed to the stable for his horse, but the horse told him that he would never get the doves back from Hansel this time, for he was riding the witch's horse whose magic was stronger than his own. The dragon bellowed, but nevertheless he mounted a horse and rode after Hansel. When he caught him up and stretched out his hand to seize the doves, the huge horse gave him such a mighty kick on the head that the dragon fell down dead.

And in this way the three princesses, who had been the doves, were delivered from their cruel spell and all the old witch's horses were likewise saved. Hansel rode home in triumph with his wife. And they lived happily ever after.

## XV

# The Shepherd Boy's Dream

ONCE upon a time there was a poor shepherd who lived in a tiny village in a remote part of the country. He had a wife and one child, a son. As soon as this little lad's legs had grown sturdy enough to let him follow his father, the shepherd used to take his son with him when he drove his sheep to their pastures up on the mountain-side. He taught him all that a good and conscientious shepherd should know and do, and by the time the boy was twelve his father was able to trust him to look after the sheep by himself and knew that they would come to no harm. This allowed the poor shepherd to earn some extra money by doing a day's work here or there, or by making baskets, at which he was very clever.

The young shepherd lad used to drive his flock up on to the high pastures on the mountain-sides, or to the low ones in the valley down by its foot; he whistled and sang and never found that time passed slowly or that the day was too long. When noon came and the sun made the world hot and sleepy, he would drive his flock together, make a little camp where he ate the bread and cheese he had brought with him, quenched his thirst from a bubbling spring and then went to sleep, until the worst of the heat was over and it was time to get the sheep on to their feet again. One hot day, as he lay in the shade of some bushes, he dreamed a wonderful dream.

He had been travelling and had gone far, endlessly far—then he heard a loud clinking as though coins were falling to the ground in a steady stream, then came a great thundering as though many guns were being fired off one after the other, and, finally, a countless host of soldiers with weapons and gleaming armour appeared and manoeuvred, circling round him with much din and shouting. He, however, just walked on and on up the mountain-side until after a long time he came to the very summit. There a throne had been built, and on this throne he seated himself. No sooner had he done so, than a beautiful woman came and took her place beside him; whereupon the shepherd boy got to his feet in the dream and in firm and solemn voice announced:

"I am the King of Spain." And the moment he said that, he woke up.

As he drove his flock home from the mountain he could not help wondering about this strange dream and what it could mean; and when he reached home and found his parents sitting outside the door of their little cottage, preparing withes for making baskets, he told them of his dream, and added:

"If I dream this dream again, I shall go away to Spain. They might make me king. You never know!"

"You silly boy," said his old father, "who would make you king! You are just being ridiculous."

## THE SHEPHERD BOY'S DREAM

And the boy's mother laughed and clapped her hands and said:

"King of Spain! King of Spain!"

The next morning the shepherd's son again drove the flock to the same part of the mountain, and when midday came he again lay down in the shade of the bushes by the same spring. And then, wonder of wonders, he dreamed the same lovely dream all over again. He could scarcely wait for the evening to drive his sheep home; in fact it was all he could do to stop himself running straight home and starting off on his journey to Spain. When at length the shadows had lengthened and he and his flock reached the village, he called out to his parents that he had had the dream again and added:

"And if I dream it once more, I am starting off without delay, at once!"

The next day he made his midday camp for the third time in the shade of the bushes by the spring, and for a third time he dreamed the dream, in which he got to his feet, puffed out his chest and said:

"I am the King of Spain."

Then he woke up. Now he no longer hesitated, but picked up his hat, his crook and his knapsack, collected his sheep and drove them, bleating protestingly, straight to the village. The villagers scolded him for bringing his flock back so early, and so did his parents, but he was so excited at having dreamed his dream a third time, that he paid no attention to their scolding, but quickly bundled up his few clothes and belongings, especially his Sunday suit, hung the bundle on a stick over his shoulder and walked off without saying goodbye to anyone. He strode along as fast as ever he could, for he was most anxious to get to Spain before nightfall. What he did reach was a forest. There seemed to be neither village nor any house in it; so, when he grew tired, he decided to find a nice thick bush, creep into it and sleep there. Scarcely had he got himself comfortable and fallen asleep, than he was awakened by a loud commotion. A group of men came marching past the clump of bushes in which he was lying, talking in loud voices. Quietly the lad crept out of the bushes and followed them at a distance, for he thought to himself: "Perhaps they will lead me to a better place in which to spend the night. Where they sleep, there will surely be room for me too."

They had not gone very far like this before they came to a magnificent house, deep in the heart of the forest. The men knocked on its stout front door, and the door was opened. Because it was dark, the shepherd lad was able to slip inside with the men without them noticing him. Then a door leading to a big room opened and they all trooped in. The room was badly lighted and most of it lay in shadow. On the floor was a number of sacks of straw and some mattresses and palliasses, which no doubt were beds for the men to sleep on. The shepherd lad swiftly crept behind a heap of straw piled up just near the door, and from this hiding-place he was able to hear and see all that went on.

He soon realized that the men were members of a robber band and that the master of the house was their captain. As soon as the men had settled themselves on their couches, the master of the house seated himself on a chair, so that he was somewhat higher than the others, and in a deep voice said:

"My good men, let me now have your reports. Tell

me all that you have done today: where you have been, what houses you have broken into and what loot you have brought back."

The first to stand up and make his report was a tall man with a coal-black beard. He said:

"Captain, this morning I robbed a nobleman of a pair of leather trousers. They are not ordinary trousers. They have two pockets and whenever you turn these inside out and shake them hard a gold coin falls to the ground."

"That sounds as though you have done well," said the Captain.

Then a second got to his feet. He was short and round and very fat, and he said:

"This morning I stole a general's three-cornered hat. This, too, is no ordinary hat, even for a general, for when you twist it round and round on your head, it keeps firing shots out of its three corners."

"That was well done," said the Captain.

Then a third stood up and said in a deep, gruff voice:

"Today I have robbed a knight of his sword. If you plunge the point of this sword into the ground, at once you will have a whole regiment of soldiers at your command."

"A noteworthy accomplishment," said the Captain, and turned to the fourth robber, who was tall and very thin, and asked what he had done.

"I have stolen a traveller's boots, and they too are no ordinary boots. If you put them on you can cover a mile in but seven strides."

"Well done, indeed," said the Captain. "Now put your things on the chair over there, then eat and drink your fill and sleep long and well." The Captain then stood up, said goodnight and left the room. The four robbers then gathered round the table and ate a mighty meal of lovely things that made the shepherd lad's mouth water, then they flung themselves down on their beds and went fast asleep.

When all was quiet and the lad felt sure that the robbers were sound asleep, he crept out of his hiding place and carefully went across to the chair. Then, taking off his own, he stepped into the leather trousers, set the hat on his head, buckled the sword round his waist, pulled on the boots and stole quietly out of the house.

Once safely outside, he stepped out with a will and the boots proved that they did indeed have magic powers, for in seven strides he covered a whole mile. He strode on and on, and it was not so very long before he reached the gates of Madrid, the capital city of Spain. Entering, he stopped the first person he saw and asked the way to the best inn in the city. The person he asked looked him up and down and said curtly:

"Come, young fellow. Go to a place where people of your sort stay, not to where the rich eat."

However, a gleaming gold coin quickly made the man more polite: in fact he offered to guide the young stranger to the very best inn. There the shepherd lad took one of the best rooms. Affably he said to the innkeeper:

"How are things in your city? What's the news?"

The innkeeper looked at him rather condescendingly:

"I see, sir, that you are a complete stranger here.

## THE SHEPHERD BOY'S DREAM

You do not seem yet to have heard that our King is arming. We have a great enemy who has mustered an army of twenty thousand men and is preparing to attack us. Oh, yes, times are bad, indeed. Would you, sir, not like to join the King's army?"

"Why, yes. I would, indeed," said the shepherd lad, his face beaming with delight.

No sooner had the innkeeper left his room than the shepherd lad took off his leather trousers and shook some gold coins out of the pockets, after which he went out into the main streets and bought himself expensive clothes, arms and jewellery. When he returned to the inn, he dressed in his new clothes, obtained a messenger and sent him to the King with a request for an audience. The messenger came back and told him that the King would see him, and when the shepherd lad went to the palace at the appointed hour, two chamberlains received him and led him through a suite of magnificent rooms. As they walked along, they met a sweet and wonderfully beautiful girl. The shepherd lad bowed to her, and she smiled graciously to the handsome young man between the two chamberlains who then whispered in the shepherd lad's ear:

"That was the Crown Princess, the King's daughter."

The shepherd lad was very struck by the beauty of the young Crown Princess. To him she seemed so lovely, that when he came to the King he was bold enough to make this proposal:

"Your Majesty! Humbly I offer my services. The Army that I shall bring to you, your Majesty, will defeat all your enemies and conquer whatever territory you may desire. Gladly will I serve you thus, but this one reward I must ask for: If I return victorious to your country and to this your capital city, then I shall be entitled to take your fair daughter home as my wife. If you will allow that, Sire, then proclaim your agreement and your will."

The King was no little surprised at this bold speech; however, he agreed and said:

"I accept your proposal. If you return the victor, you shall be my successor, and you shall have my daughter as your wife."

Then the shepherd lad went out into the fields outside the city altogether, and there he stuck his sword repeatedly into the earth. Within a few minutes a great host of several thousand soldiers, armed and accoutred, was standing there: while the shepherd lad, now dressed as a commander, was mounted on a white charger with a saddle-cloth embroidered with gold and a bridle that was studded with jewels. At the head of a seemingly endless column of his men, the young commander now rode against the enemy. There was a great and gory battle in which the commander's hat shot a stream of mortal bullets from its three corners, while the magic sword kept conjuring up more and more reinforcements. In a few hours the enemy was soundly defeated and his army scattered to the four winds. News of the victory spread like wildfire throughout the country and flags were hoisted and church bells rung in all the towns and villages. But the youthful commander pursued the retreating enemy and took from him the most valuable part of his country.

Victorious, his name covered with glory, the shepherd lad marched back to Madrid, where the best part of his good fortune still awaited him. The lovely young princess was just as enchanted by the slim and handsome young commander as he was by her. Her father, the King, was well aware how great were the services this young man had rendered him and gladly fulfilled the promise he had made. Thus the princess became the shepherd lad's bride and the successor to the throne.

Their wedding was a great and very magnificent occasion. He who had been a shepherd lad could scarcely believe his good fortune. A short time later the old King laid aside his crown and transferred everything, his crown, his sceptre, his duties and his rights, to his son-in-law. So there the new King sat enthroned with his wife beside him, while the people paid homage to their new lord.

That evening, as the new King sat at table with his young wife, he remembered the dream he had dreamed three times on the mountain-side, and how it had all come true; then, too, he remembered his parents and how poor they were, and he said to his wife:

"Beloved, my parents are still alive. They live far from here and they are very poor. My father is a village shepherd and I too used to help look after the sheep. Then it was made known to me in a wonderful dream, most wonderfully repeated, that one day I should become King of Spain. Fortune has been with me, and, see, now I am become King of Spain and you my bride. Nonetheless, I would like to see my poor parents made happy for once in their lives, and so I ask you to agree to my going home to fetch them and to their coming to live here."

The Queen of course was only too glad for him to go and fetch his parents. Having his magic boots, the journey did not take the young King long. On the way he stopped and gave all the magic things he had taken from the robbers back to their rightful owners; all, that is, except the boots, and in exchange for these he gave the traveller a whole duchy. So he lived happily and worthily as King of Spain until the end of his days.

## XVI

# Little Earthworm

PEASANT KUNZ and his wife Katherine had a big family. The nicest of their nice children was their youngest daughter, Eva Maria. Eva was quiet and rather shy; she liked being alone in the solitude of their garden and of the green forest. Nature she loved. At the age of ten little Eva knew almost all about the animals, birds, flowers and trees of those parts. She was at home with them and they with her, as though they had known each other for a hundred years. She was almost as fond of brightly coloured stones and was delighted when she found one. She could play all day long with ladybirds, rose-bugs, butterflies and tree-frogs and never think the hours long. When she was eleven she had to start looking after her parents' cows while they grazed in the forest. There she always managed to collect a surprising number of things, and when she returned home in the evening, her pockets would be full of coloured stones and little boxes and baskets she had made herself and in which she had put beetles, butterflies and Heaven knows what besides. Because of her interest in stones and beetles and such things, Eva was always rummaging in the soil, turning over sticks and stones and peeling bits of bark off trees, and in the end everyone called her Little Earthworm.

One day, when Eva was twelve, she drove her cows and calves into the forest as usual, and there she met an old woman. The poor old woman's clothes were so tattered and torn that she was almost naked, and she looked very pale and ill. She complained bitterly of the cold. Eva could not bear to see her thus, and she took off her own dress and hung it round the old woman. As she went on her way, the old woman called out: "Thank you, my child. This shall not go unrewarded." All that day Eva went about in just her bodice and was very cold, and in the evening her mother gave her a bad scolding for giving away more than they could afford, for now they had to buy Eva a new dress.

When summer had come and days were long and hot, Eva used to bathe in the pond in the forest. One day as she came out and went to get her clothes from the bush behind which she had undressed, she found not her own old clothes, but lovely new ones of beautiful material and a pair of new shoes.

"Oh, who can have given me these lovely clothes," exclaimed Eva.

"I have," said the old woman to whom Eva had once given her dress, suddenly appearing. "I have given you them, because you were so kind to an old woman. Now, tell me, is there anything else you would like?"

Eva thought for a moment, and then said: "If you could have that lovely shiny golden beetle come and play with me every day; the one I have seen here only once and could not catch."

"I am not surprised you couldn't catch him, for he

**LITTLE EARTHWORM**

is a very tricky customer," said the old woman. "But he shall come. Goodbye."

Scarcely had the old woman disappeared from sight than Eva heard a buzz! buzz! and through the trees came a big, gleaming golden beetle and landed beside her. Its wings were like gold and its two bright eyes sparkled like diamonds. Eva played with it all the rest of that day. When the time came for her to drive her herd home, the beetle spread its little wings and flew off.

Every day that Eva was in the forest, the beetle came and stayed with her till it was time for her to go home. One day when they were together under the green oak that was Eva's favourite place, a lovely ladybird she had there suddenly spread its little wings and in an instant was over the oak and away.

"Oh, if only I could fly like that," Eva exclaimed.

"Would you really like to?" said the beetle.

"Oh, yes, indeed!" said Eva, and the next instant the sweetest little coach came flying through the air and landed at Eva's feet.

"If you want to fly, step in," said the beetle.

The coach was delicately made of the finest ivory and had innumerable tiny birds and flowers carved and painted on it. It was large enough for a little girl to be able to sit in it comfortably and was drawn by six sky-blue dragonflies. Eva clapped her hands with delight. "Step in," said the beetle; but Eva just laughed for she could not believe that six dragonflies could draw a sturdy little girl like her. "Step in," repeated the beetle, "if you want to fly." And more for a joke than anything else Eva stepped in. The beetle swung itself onto the box, picked up the reins, cracked the golden whip, the lash of which was spun of the finest sunbeams, and the six dragonflies plunged forward and up they soared over the tall oaks and

They were over the trees and away and Eva

beeches and away over the forest. Eva, who had never thought it was anything but a joke, was rather frightened and wanted to cry out: "Stop! Stop!" only it was already too late. They were over the trees and away, and she was too busy hanging on to do or say anything. She soon saw that there was no danger and began to enjoy the flight immensely. They sped on and

was too busy hanging on to say anything.

on till they had gone a good ten miles across the forest, and then the golden beetle turned the dragonflies and back they flew to where Eva's cows were, landing in the very same spot from which they had taken off.

After that Eva often used her dragonfly coach and sometimes raced hawks and pigeons and other swift-flying birds. Sometimes too, the beetle would invite her to a night flight, and then she would steal out of bed when the others were all asleep and slip out of the house to her waiting coach. She loved those trips by moon- and star-light best of all.

So it went on every year till Eva was sixteen. Though so old, she still herded the cows in the forest, and there one day the beetle, who came to her less often now, appeared with the coach and told her that there was the loveliest rainbow in the sky and suggested that she should go and look at it from near by. Eva stepped in; her coachman cracked his whip and off they flew.

They went so fast that the sky and the forest was just a blur. Eva had to hang on for dear life and saw not a sign of the lovely rainbow she had been promised. The beetle cracked his whip, the dragonflies strained themselves to the utmost and the wind blew so hard in Eva's face that she could scarcely breathe. After what seemed a long time, the coach began to descend and then landed in quite unfamiliar surroundings. Eva stepped out and was just turning round to ask "Where are we?" when her coach, driver and horses took off again and flew away.

It was already night, but the moon and stars shed some light. Poor Eva clenched her fists and wanted to cry, but feeling that she ought to try to walk home, she set off bravely through the bushes. She was so tired, however, that soon she had to give up, and, lying down, she fell asleep.

When Eva awoke, the sun was already high in the

sky. She looked round in amazement, then remembered the crazy flight, and realized that she had no idea where she was. All round were high mountains, their peaks white with snow, and poor Eva felt that she would never be able to get home or see her dear parents again, and she bitterly regretted having gone with the beetle. She began to walk and soon came to a little orchard. Being very hungry she went in and picked and ate some pears and apples that hung on the trees. Feeling better, she walked on, then all at once she heard a cock crow and a dog bark. Those familiar sounds made her feel much happier and she walked on more quickly. Then a sweet little house with a thatched roof came into view and she went towards it. A dog came running up to her, wagging its tail, barking joyfully and jumping up; then a snow-white cat appeared and rubbed against her leg, purring loudly, and both accompanied her to the house.

By the door of the little house sat an old woman singing as she spun. It was a song that Eva knew and loved, so she joined in too, and the two sang it together to the end. Then the old woman stood up and bade Eva welcome, calling her by her name. Eva was very surprised, but looking at the old woman she recognized her as the one she had met in the forest and who had sent her the beetle coach. Then Eva told the old woman how the beetle had deceived her with promises of a lovely rainbow and then brought her to this place, where she had no idea where she was, and left her without a word of explanation. Eva, in fact, was quite angry with her coachman, but she was also very pleased to see the old woman and told her so and asked her to tell her the way through the mountains to her home and her parents, who must be dreadfully worried, she said, at her failing to come home.

"You are very welcome here, Eva," said the old woman. "Your parents' house is very far away and I cannot take you there now. The roads are all unsafe, because war has broken out, and yesterday enemy soldiers reached the village where you live. That is why your coachmen fetched you and brought you here. You could not have helped your parents in any way, while you yourself might have suffered in all sorts of ways. So just resign yourself and stay with me here. This house is nicely tucked away in the forest, and here we are safe. No enemy will ever cross those snow mountains. When things are quiet again and peace is restored, I will take you back home."

So Eva agreed and stayed with the old woman in her thatched house in the forest, and though she was very comfortable and well looked after, she often cried at the thought of her parents and how worried they must be and the awful things that the war might do to them.

The house was really a farm-house, and there was a little farm all by itself there in the forest. They had several fields, a garden, a pasture and plenty of wood. In the ponds and streams in the forest were carp and trout. Here the old woman lived with her old husband, who must have been older even than she, and a farmhand who was far from young. Together the three ran the farm. They had two oxen, two horses, eight cows, twenty sheep and goats, and lots of hens and ducks. The garden gave them fruit and vegetables, the fields corn for their bread, and so they lived well and happily. Eva, of course, was able to help them. In the summer, there was lots for them all to do, and in winter, while the two men threshed the corn and fetched wood and logs from the forest, the old woman and Eva would sit down to their spinning-wheels as soon as they had seen to the cows and the kitchens, and spin yarn while they chatted and told each other stories.

Five years passed; it seemed to Eva, in a flash. Then, one fine morning, the old woman came into Eva's room and said: "Eva dear, the time has come for you to leave and go back to your parents. Their village has suffered greatly, as has the whole country, but now the war is over and peace is restored, and it is right for you to go back and help. I had you brought here, not just because I am very fond of you, as you know, but to save you from the savagery of war. Now that the danger is gone, I cannot keep you from your parents. You will have realized that I have various arts, but I use them only for good. So, think only well of me, I am one of those whom people call good wise women, and I have spent my life turning wrong into right. Now dear girl, get your things together and pack your clothes, for tomorrow we shall go."

The following morning, the waggon with the two horses pulled up at the door. Eva and the old woman got in; the farmhand drove. They travelled for six days, and on the seventh day they came to the big village next to that where Eva's parents lived. The old woman stopped the cart at the inn and said to Eva: "Now, I must say goodbye, my child; I can go no further. God bless you." Then she had the farmhand unload Eva's luggage, and into Eva's hand she put a purse, saying: "There, my child; that shall be your dowry; with it you can buy a little farm." Then the old woman drove off, leaving Eva at the inn. She got the innkeeper to harness his horse and drive her to the next village.

As they drew near the village, Eva was surprised to see so few houses and that some of these were quite new. She even asked if it were the right village, and was assured that it was, only that in the war many of the houses had been burned and people were now rebuilding them. Eva was frightened, as she thought of what might have happened to her parents, and she did not dare ask about them. Soon they reached the village, where were many black places where houses had been burned, broken fences and tumbled walls. So she reached her father's house. It too was new. There she found her father and mother alive and well. You can imagine their joy at having their dear daughter back again safe and sound, when they had given her up for lost. The war had left Eva's parents very poor, but they still had plenty of courage. All her brothers and sisters were alive too, except for one brother who had fallen in the war, but her two sisters had married and were living in other villages.

Then Eva told her wonderful story, and how now she was able to help them, saying which she opened her purse and in it found five hundred golden ducats.

It was not long before Eva married, and in time she had a family of her own. She taught all her children to love and be kind to all animals, birds and insects, but strangely enough she thought it best that they should not go flying in dragonfly coaches.

## XVII

# The Wolf and the Nightingale

IN the olden days when things were quite different from what they are now, there was once a King whose Queen was the loveliest of all queens in the world and they had two children, a son and a daughter. The Queen died when the two children were still quite young and the King mourned her long; but when the children were nearly grown up the King married again. The new Queen was a wicked woman, and she was not kind at all to her step-children, though the young prince and princess were nice, pleasant children and very well-behaved. The people hated the new Queen and whenever she went anywhere with the young princess, they cheered the princess and called out: "She is as lovely as her mother was," but they never cheered the Queen. That, of course, made her bitter and angry, and she came to hate her step-daughter, though of course she dare not show it.

Time passed and the princess, whose name was Aurora, became lovelier and lovelier. Many suitors came to ask for her hand, but she would listen to none of them till the Prince of the East came to her father's court, and he was the right one. They became engaged and Princess Aurora was happier and lovelier than she had ever been, and the Queen hated her more and more. The Queen, in fact, was determined to spite the princess and prevent her from enjoying her happiness. She tried many tricks, but none succeeded, for the princess and her brother were too well guarded by their servants and by the ladies and gentlemen of their suite, who never left them day or night, and who loved them for their own and their mother's sake.

The day came for the princess to be married and still the Queen had not accomplished her evil design. With no time left, she had recourse to a desperate expedient. On the princess's very wedding morning she went to her, and, smiling her sweetest and falsest smile, asked her and her brother to come to the rose garden to look at a particularly lovely rose that had just come out. The two went with the Queen, for the garden lay just behind the palace; also it was in the middle of a sunny morning, the King was there and the palace was full of guests come for the wedding, so who could have suspected anything? The Queen led the prince and princess to the far corner of the garden where her roses were and into the dark shadow beneath an old yew tree, pretending that she had something to show them. There she softly murmured a few words, broke off a twig of yew and with it three times gently stroked the back first of the prince, then of the princess. At once prince and princess were turned into animals: the prince became a wolf and leaped over the wall and ran off into the forest, while the princess became a little grey bird, a nightingale, which flew up into a tree where it began to sing most sadly.

The Queen played her part so well that no one suspected anything. She ran screaming to the palace, where she collapsed in a faint on the steps leading to the great hall. Her women came and carried her to her bed, and it was a quarter of an hour before she came to. Then she moaned and lamented and told them that a lot of brigands had suddenly swarmed over the wall, seized hold of the two children and carried them off knocking the Queen herself to the ground and leaving her for dead. She showed them a great lump on her head, which she had purposely made by banging against the trunk of a tree, and everyone believed her.

The King ordered his nobles and gentlemen to pursue the brigands. Quickly they mounted their horses and rode off. They combed the forest and searched the hills and valleys for several miles around, but they could find no trace of either the brigands or the princess and her brother. The King would not rest, but kept up the search for weeks and months, even sending messengers and envoys to neighbouring countries and other lands; yet they too came back without news. It was as though Aurora and her brother had never existed. The King, however, believed that the brigands had seized them for the sake of the jewels they were wearing for the wedding and that, having robbed them, they had killed them and buried them somewhere in the forest. He was so broken-hearted that he soon died. As he lay dying, he said that, since his children had disappeared, the Queen must rule the country, and he asked his people to obey her; this they did, if only out of love for the dead king.

Four years passed. The Queen ruled her people

harshly. She sold the jewels the King had left her and sent for foreign soldiers to come and guard her and the palace, and day by day the people hated her more and more, for she was a wicked woman and anyone who even whispered anything about her was put to death. The Queen was sure that the princess and her brother would remain the bird and wolf into which her wicked spell had transformed them, leaving her to enjoy her power and the throne; but things turned out quite differently.

The poor children were not at all happy. The young prince had to behave like a wolf. He had to howl like a wolf and day and night roam the wild and desolate places, as a wolf must; and he had to slink and crawl like a thief, for the fear that wolves have, had also entered into him. He had to feed himself as other wolves did, and in winter he often had to curl up with empty belly and chattering teeth among hard, cold stones. But there was one strange thing about this wolf, he only attacked and ate animals, and never went for people, though I am sure he must have thirsted for the blood of the wicked woman who had turned him into a wolf. You must not think that he still thought and felt like a prince, no, he was a wolf and thought and behaved like one, except that some strange urge and dark longing kept driving him back to that part of the forest near the palace and its garden. And every time he turned his face towards the palace, he felt strangely savage, yet each time when he came within a thousand paces of the palace, a cold shiver ran through him and something forced him to halt and turn back. That was the Queen's magic. She could keep him at that distance, but further than that her powers did not reach.

## THE WOLF AND THE NIGHTINGALE

Nor was the Queen content to let him be a wolf; she wanted to kill him and so she arranged many wolf hunts in the forest round the palace, but always this particular wolf managed to escape.

Princess Aurora had been turned into a nightingale, but she remembered far more than her brother, the wolf, and many of her thoughts and feelings were almost human. In her loneliness she sang all the more beautifully because she was unable to speak. The animals used to gather to listen to her, and they would jump and leap for joy; and the birds would come flying to hear her and settled in such numbers that the boughs bent and the flowers all nodded.

The wicked Queen wanted to kill the nightingale too. As a result, in those days it was a great misfortune to be a bird and live anywhere near the palace, for after the old King's death the Queen pretended to have fallen victim to some strange sickness that made not only the cawing and screeching of the bigger birds intolerable to her, but also the twittering and singing of the little song-birds. To make people believe this, she once or twice pretended to faint when the air was loud with birdsong that delighted everyone but her. And so the Queen declared war on all birds, so that not only the little nightingale-princess was in danger, but all other birds as well. All the foresters and rangers had the strictest orders to hunt everything that wore feathers; they were not allowed to spare even robins or wrens, at which no one would ever wish to shoot. The canaries and other birds that people kept in their houses were ordered to be killed; and as a result thousands of canaries and siskins, nightingales and goldfinches, even parrots and cockatoos, were slaughtered. Even farmyard poultry were not spared, and hens became as rare as Chinese pheasants.

Because of all this people stopped going for walks in the forest, and so no one heard the nightingale singing her lovely songs, except perhaps a passing ranger and he would pretend not to hear, so that the Queen could not say to him: "Why did you not shoot it?"

Though she could not bring herself to leave the forest near the palace for long, and always returned when the horns and guns of the hunters had forced her to take flight, the little nightingale managed to survive. But do not think that she was always sad. She liked living in the green wood among all the bright little flowers and she found pleasure in singing as sweetly as she could for the moon and the stars. It was only when autumn came and forced her to leave with the other nightingales and go to foreign lands until spring returned, that she was really unhappy.

The little nightingale-princess lived mostly in a thick green oak that leaned out over a rippling stream on the bank of which she and her betrothed, the prince, had whispered many words of love to each other. Here she often saw the wolf who came, driven by his dark urge to seek the neighbourhood of the palace. She did not know that he was her brother, but she grew fond of him, because he so often lay down, stretched out and listened to her song, as though he understood some of what she was saying. And at times she felt sorry for the wolf, because he had to be fierce and savage and could not flit from branch to branch as she and other birds could.

There was one man, however, who did hear the song

of the little nightingale. This was the Prince of the East, the man the princess had been going to marry. The old King had loved and admired the Prince, and on his deathbed he had commended him to the Queen as an adviser and helper and as a commander for her forces. And out of love for the old King, the Prince of the East had stayed at the palace with the Queen, but he soon saw that she hated him and that she wanted to kill him, so he had left and gone to his own home, back to his father's country, which lay many hundreds of miles to the east. After that the Queen proclaimed him outlaw, which meant that anyone might kill him, and set a great price on his head.

So the Prince lived with his father, but he was ever restless and the ache of grief for the vanished princess never left him. And every year he went secretly away, no one knew where. He would saddle his horse, put on a suit of ordinary armour and ride off. It was to the wicked Queen's country that he went, for something impelled him to visit the forest in which the princess had vanished. This great and irresistible urge came to him each year shortly before the time of the princess's disappearance, when it sent him galloping through wild and desolate country till he came to the familiar places where he and the princess had walked and ridden together. Perhaps their favourite place of all had been the bank of the stream by the overhanging oak, and there the Prince spent fourteen nights weeping and praying and lamenting his beloved. The days he spent hiding in the depths of the thicket. There he often saw the little nightingale and listened to her lovely song, and the nightingale saw him; but neither realized who the other was. The little bird always felt a great yearning when the man had ridden away again, but she did not know why, and for a long time afterwards her song would be sad.

The sixth year came since the princess and her brother had vanished. The Queen still lived in the palace doing as she liked, having the animals hunted and the birds shot, and being no less harsh to her own subjects. She thought herself all-powerful and that nothing could happen to her; yet since the day when she had changed the princess and her brother into bird and wolf, she had never set foot in the forest, nor even in the rose garden. Now, in the sixth year, she decided to give a great feast. All the princes and princesses of neighbouring countries were invited and the nobles of her own land. For the afternoon a wolf hunt was arranged and the princes all asked her to join in it. For a long time she refused, making all sorts of pretexts, but in the end she let herself be persuaded. She mounted a tall carriage and had three of her bravest officers come and sit beside her. She ordered several hundred of her guards to ride in front and behind and on either side of her, and a long line of coaches with the ladies and gentlemen of her court followed along behind. Though secretly still afraid of the wolf, she said to herself: let him come. Let a hundred wolves come, my brave soldiers will deal with them. But her time was up, as other masters of her black art had warned her. They told her to beware of the sixth year, but she had forgotten their warning.

It was a lovely, warm spring day. The great company rode into the forest with trumpets blowing and horses whinnying, armour clanking and the sunlight glinting on spears and swords. Before very long, the hunt turned in the direction of the Queen: the sound of the huntsmen's horns, the baying of the hounds and the shouts of the riders grew nearer and nearer. A bear came galloping along; then a wild boar. They charged the line of the Queen's guards, and the guards killed them both. But then came what was too much even for the guards. A terrifying wolf came bounding out of the thicket into the open, where it howled so horribly that everybody's blood ran cold. Then the wolf too charged—it ran, no, it flew through the ranks of men and horses, and the men all forgot that they had swords and spears and arrows, and no one moved. Straight as an arrow the wolf made for the Queen's carriage. She saw it coming and cried out: "Help, help!" Her women screamed and fainted, and many of the men even turned pale and trembled. No one tried to stop the wolf which made with long bounds straight for the Queen's carriage, leaped up and dragged her to the ground where it plunged its teeth into her throat and worried it.

Then, as the men came to themselves and made to attack the wolf, there was no wolf to be seen. Instead, a handsome, stalwart young man stood where the wolf had been. People rubbed their eyes, but some still drew their swords and moved forward as though to attack the young man. All at once a grey-haired old man came running out and cried to them to stop, that they did not know whom they were attacking. Then, before any realized what he meant, the old man had kneeled down before the young stranger and taken his hand and kissed it. Then the old man, who was the Chancellor, called out: "Rejoice, people, the King's son has come back. He is now your King." At that others came running up and recognized the young prince and paid homage to him. And everybody was much surprised and rather over-awed and at the same time they wanted to rejoice, and they had so much else to think about that they forgot about the old Queen and the wolf, for no one yet realized that the prince had been the wolf.

The young King called off the hunt and invited everyone to accompany him back to his father's palace. There, in those once familiar surroundings, the prince suddenly became aware of all that had happened to him, and he told the Chancellor and the nobles how his stepmother had turned him into a wolf, and how it was only the magic power of her blood that had turned him back again. The news of this spread like wildfire and everyone was overjoyed to have the young prince back safe and sound, and also that the hated Queen had been killed.

Happy though the young King was to be human again, his heart was sad when he thought of his dear sister, Aurora, and he wondered whether she might not have been turned into some animal too. He questioned everyone, but no one could tell him more than that she had vanished at the same time as he.

It so happened that on the day of the great wolf hunt that had restored the prince to human shape, the poor, grieving Prince of the East had been hiding in his thicket near the overhanging oak, among the green leaves of which the little nightingale had sat silent and hidden. The strangest thrill had coursed through the bird's little heart as the wolf's greedy teeth sank into the wicked old Queen's throat. Then, when the noise of the hunt had drawn away and fallen silent, after the new King had called it off, the Prince had emerged from his thicket and gone and leaned sadly against the trunk of the oak. Then all at once the nightingale in the branches above had begun to sing, and it seemed to the Prince that its song was quite different, puzzling and as though it had meaning, almost human. And the Prince shivered, as though he were afraid, and called up to the bird: "Nightingale, tell me, can you speak?" And the little nightingale answered "Yes," as a person would, and was itself amazed to find that it could speak.

Then the nightingale began to weep with joy, but after a while it began again to speak in a human voice and told the Prince the whole story of how she and her brother had been transformed by the wicked Queen, and of the miracle by which her brother had become human again. For she suddenly knew all that had happened, as though a spirit had whispered it into her ear. The man's heart leaped for joy as he heard her tale, and he wondered what next to do. Meanwhile, the little bird flew about him most trustingly, yet though she knew all that had happened to herself and her brother, strangely enough she did not recognize the man or know who he was. He petted and cosseted the bird and asked it to come home with him, promising to put it in a garden which spring never left and where there were no hawks, and hunters never came; it would be much nicer, he said, than living in the forest and having to fear the winter and hunters and birds of prey. But the nightingale would not hear of it, but said it preferred its oak and the forest, and meanwhile it fluttered round the man, twittering and singing and playing most trustingly.

All at once the man seized the bird by its little feet,

ran to his horse, leaped into the saddle and rode off at a gallop, making for an inn of which he knew in the town, not far from the palace. There he asked for a secluded room in which he shut himself up with the nightingale. When the bird saw how he took the key from the door and turned the room into a prison, it began to weep most pitiably and begged him to let it go. But the Prince paid no attention to its entreaties, so then the little bird became angry and began to assume different shapes in order to frighten the man into opening the door or window. First, it turned itself into a tiger, then into a lion, then into an otter, and after that into a snake, a scorpion, a tarantula and, last of all, a horrible dragon that twined round the man and licked him with its venomous tongue; but the man was not frightened and would not give way, and, having had all that trouble for nothing, the nightingale had to turn itself back into a bird again. The man, however, was deep in thought, trying to remember an old tale he had been told in his childhood. Then he took a knife from his pocket and made a small cut in the little finger of his left hand, where the best blood always is. Then he took some of the blood that dripped out and with it smeared the little bird's head and body. No sooner had he done that than the nightingale turned into a lovely girl, the Princess Aurora, who now recognized the young man as her betrothed.

Princess Aurora was as young and lovely as she had been six years before, for it is a strange thing about magic that when people are transformed, the years which they spend in their different shape do not age them at all, not even if it be a thousand years.

## THE WOLF AND THE NIGHTINGALE

You can imagine how overjoyed the two were to be together again. After a while they sent word to the King, that two princes had come from afar and requested the hospitality of his court. The King sent for them to come and when he saw them, he recognized his sister, Aurora, and the man she was to have married, the Prince of the East. And everybody was overjoyed.

A few days later the new King was crowned and began to rule in his father's stead. He gave his sister a magnificent wedding. She asked her brother for that part of the forest in which she had lived as a nightingale and experienced so many joys and sorrows, and gladly he gave it to her. There she and her husband built a proud little castle. The overhanging oak was right in the middle of the castle's garden and lived so long that Princess Aurora's grandchildren's grandchildren played in its shade. The Princess decreed that the forest should remain in its natural state for all time, and it was most strictly forbidden to shoot or net birds, or to set snares for birds or animals, anywhere within its confines.

Thenceforth it became traditional that the eldest boy of each generation was named Rossignol and the first girl, Philomela, so that they should always remember how their ancestor, the Princess Aurora, had been transformed into a nightingale for six long years.

## XVIII

# The Christmas Present

ONCE upon a time there lived a stocking-weaver, called Paul Nicholas, with his wife and six children. There were three boys and three girls. The boys had dark hair and light eyes, like their mother, and the girls had chestnut hair and deep blue eyes, like their father. They were a very happy family because they all loved one another and helped each other, but there was not always enough work for the weaver and they were very, very poor. Sometimes they even went short of food and they were never able to have nice clothes or toys, like the children of richer parents. However, they were never envious or sad, and they certainly never complained. Each one of the family did his or her best to help to make life easier for the others. The girls helped their mother in the house, and the boys went off into the forest to collect firewood. In the summer and autumn they would all go out and pick mushrooms and nuts and blackberries which they sold in the town. The boys also did odd jobs for some of the farmers in the neighbourhood, which earned them a little money and helped buy food for the rest of the family.

Winter was the worst time of all the year for the weaver and his family, everything cost more money and work was scarcer to find. One winter, just before Christmas, the weaver had set his heart on giving some little treat to his wife and children at a time when everyone should be merry and glad. He had worked extra hard at his loom, trudged many long journeys into the towns to try to sell his stockings, but he met with little success. He scarcely earned enough money to keep his poor family from starving, let alone to give them presents or treats. He could not bear to think of them having to watch the beautiful Christmas trees being carried into their neighbours' houses, and to see the sparkling trinkets and toys in the shop windows, knowing that there would be none in their home that Christmas Eve.

The children would see others making merry and feasting all around, while they might even have to go hungry. Paul knew that they would not grumble, but his eyes filled with tears when he realized that he could do so little for his good, uncomplaining family.

Perhaps you can imagine his relief and joy when, just two weeks before Christmas, he was given an order by a merchant for as many stockings as he could weave by Christmas Eve. He hurried home with the good news, and how happy and excited the children all were, when he told them about his stroke of good fortune and how it meant that he would have enough money to give them a delicious Christmas dinner and a Christmas tree hung with presents for them all. They jumped and shouted and laughed, for never had they known the promise of so many good things, and that just when their luck seemed to be most against them. For the next week or more Paul hardly ate or slept he worked so hard and such long hours, so as to have a huge sackful of stockings to take to the merchant in the town. When the time came for him to set out, he told the boys to fetch a big fir branch from the forest for their Christmas tree and he promised that he would bring back presents for them all and a goose for their Christmas dinner. They all stood at the door of the cottage and watched him trudge off down the lane with the bulging sack thrown over his shoulder.

It was a lovely winter's day. Thick, crisp snow on the ground and a frosty clear blue sky above, from which the sun shone down on the weaver as he swung along, so happy at the thought of the treats in store for his family that he forgot his sack was heavy and the road long, and he never felt tired at all. He only stopped once at a farm where he saw a fine fat goose in the yard and asked the farmer how much money he wanted for it. The farmer could see that Paul was a poor man, and as he was in a kindly, Christmassy mood he said he would let him have it very cheap. The weaver explained that he would have plenty of money to pay for it on his way back from town and that he would collect it then to take home for his family's Christmas dinner. "Won't they have a feast!" he smiled to himself as he walked on towards the town faster than ever.

When he reached the town, he went straight to the merchant's house, but there he found to his grief and horror, that the merchant was not at home. He had gone away only an hour earlier and his clerk told Paul that he must come back for his money three days later, when the merchant would have returned home.

The poor weaver was numb with dismay. He begged the clerk for a small part of the money that was owing to him so that at least he could buy some bread for his hungry children, but the clerk said he had no money with which to pay him and that he must just wait three days. "Where has your master gone?" asked Paul, "perhaps if I hurry I may overtake him?" The clerk replied that his master had ridden away on his fastest horse and that no one could possibly catch him up on foot.

Then, indeed, the weaver's heart sank, and he realized he could gain nothing by asking any more questions. He took up his empty sack and turned his face homewards. How the day had changed! The morning that had been so sunny and bright had given way to a gloomy late afternoon. Clouds had covered the sun, and the sky, that had been so sparkling and blue, was like lead. As dull and heavy as the poor weaver's heart. At last, he began to realize how tired he was, and he plodded along thinking of the eager faces waiting for him at home and wondering how he was ever going to break the news to them and see their disappointment, when they realized that instead of a feast and nice presents, they were to go to bed without any supper and without one little toy to hang on their bare Christmas tree.

His mind was so filled with these sad thoughts that he never noticed how late it was and how dark it had grown in the forest, until suddenly his attention was caught by some bright little lights shining through the trees. Greatly surprised at this strange sight he left the path and walked towards the lights until he came to a clearing round which dozens of shining little lanterns were hung from the branches of the trees, as well as hundreds of apples and pears and nuts and sweets and toys. As Paul stood there, with his mouth hanging open with astonishment, a little gentleman—quite the smallest little gentleman he had ever seen—came up to him. He was most beautifully and elegantly dressed in expensive furs, with red leather boots and a cap made from the skin of a white mouse! He was no more than a foot high and so very unusual that the weaver did not know whether to laugh or to be afraid.

The tiny man bowed politely and said "You are Paul, the weaver, and we know that you are hungry and tired and sad, because you have nothing to take home to your wife and children for Christmas—and very nice children they are too, *particularly* the young ladies!" The weaver had never heard his little girls called young ladies before, so he took off his hat to the small gentleman and thanked him for the compliment.

"Now," said the little man, "you must have some refreshment, for you will need all your strength for the journey home, as that sack of yours is going to be full and heavy." He led Paul to a little shelter made of tree bark and fir branches where a small fire burnt brightly and a small table was laid with a snowy white cloth and beside it stood a chair made from a tree root. On the table was a bottle of wine and a covered plate from which came the most perfectly delicious smell. The little man nodded to the table and said to Paul: "Eat!" Greatly wondering, the weaver sat down and uncovered the dish. He needed no more encouragement, for although he had no idea of what the dish was made—except that it had a strong flavour of hare and mushrooms and rich brown gravy—he knew that he had never tasted anything so wonderfully delicious in all his life.

## THE CHRISTMAS PRESENT

"Drink!" said the little man, pointing to the bottle, and Paul poured out a glass of sparkling ruby-red wine for himself and raised it to his lips. He was just about to drink when he paused to ask "Please tell me your name, kind sir, so that I may drink to your health?" "Drink to your family at home first," replied the little man, "and then I will tell you my name."

Paul gladly drank to his wife and their six children. "And now you may drink to me," said the strange little man with a grave smile. "My name is Count Charles Goodfriend."

The weaver drank the Count's health and felt the good red wine warm and cheer him, then he rose to his feet, wished the little man a merry Christmas and thanked him most gratefully for all his kindness and hospitality.

"Wait, wait a moment," said the little Count, "do you think you could manage to carry something in that sack of yours?" The weaver thought that he could, and the Count led the way to the trees which were hung with so many good things. "Take as many of these as your sack will hold," said the little Count, "but if you will let me give you some advice, I should take mostly apples and pears." The weaver did as he was asked and not wishing to seem too greedy or to disobey the Count's request he did take more apples and pears than any of the other things, though he also found room for a good many sweets and toys as well. When his sack was stuffed full he hoisted it onto his back with many words of thanks to the kind little man, and just as he was leaving Count Goodfriend spoke a few more words of advice to him.

"Take care of what you have got and make good

use of it, for it is a reward to you and your wife and children for being kind to one another and to other people, and for not complaining about your hard lives."

As the little man stopped speaking the lights among the trees suddenly faded and went out, and the weaver found himself alone in the darkness. If it had not been for the full and heavy sack on his back he might have wondered if the whole thing had not been a dream. He found his way back to the road and set off towards home briskly and happily. He was so pleased at having so many nice things for the children that he didn't mind the weight on his back, although in some strange way it seemed to grow heavier with every step. But as he reached the outskirts of his village, the sack had really grown so enormously heavy that he had to set it down and ask a passer-by to help him carry it. After a little while the sack had become even heavier and was too much for the two of them, so that they asked another passer-by to help them. A little further still and the three of them could scarcely stagger along with this enormous load and they were obliged to ask a fourth person to help them carry it. At last the four men, panting and struggling reached the weaver's house and dumped the sack down by the door. Paul thanked his helpers warmly and they all went off wishing each other a merry Christmas. The children and their mother were gazing out of the window, their eyes round with astonishment and they all came rushing out to Paul to ask however many good things he had brought in his sack that had needed four men to carry it. The weaver called out merrily "Come along and have a look for yourselves—there are nuts and sweets and apples and pears and toys and cakes——" The children opened up the sack and nuts, cakes, sweets and toys were there, but wonder of wonders—all the apples and pears had turned into gold and silver money!

They were all speechless with amazement, then they all laughed and shouted as they saw the great glittering pile of money.

The weaver told his family all about this strange meeting with Count Goodfriend, and he did not forget to say what the little man had told him about making good use of his present. "If we want our good luck to continue and this treasure to bring us the blessings of happiness as well as wealth, then the first thing we must do is to find someone less fortunate than ourselves and bring them some happiness too." The children were delighted to think of helping other people, and they found twenty poor children who would have gone dinnerless and gave them a feast on Christmas Day that they remembered all their lives.

Paul, the weaver, continued to use his fairy-given fortune so kindly and so wisely that he became first a famous stocking-weaver, then a rich merchant and finally the mayor of his town. In spite of his high position he never ceased to help and think of those people who had less than himself. He and his wife and their children and grandchildren were always kind and loving to each other, and eager to help any poor honest people who had not been lucky enough to make the acquaintance of Count Charles Goodfriend.